Victor Valley
to
West Point
Keep Your Eyes on the Prize

By

C.A. Henderson

Victor Valley to West Point

Email: VictorValleytoWestPoint@gmail.com

www.VictorValleytoWestPoint.com

www.CAHenderson.net

Instagram *@C.A.Henderson*   **Twitter** *@CA_Thelife*

For bookings email: BookAuthorCAHenderson@gmail.com

ISBN-13: 978-0692404409

ISBN-10: 0692404406

Printed in the United States of America

Dedication

I most humbly and graciously dedicate this book to my mother and father. My mother, a scholarly woman, faithful and full of perseverance, taught me the importance of time, affection, patience, love and life. My father, industrious and ingenious, taught me the importance of Manhood and Perseverance. May their lessons of love, joy and responsibility forever enrich the lives of our legacy and community!

In Loving Memory of my father, Papa Jerry, who I had the absolute pleasure of informing that this book was dedicated to him before he passed. He will forever live through me— mind, body and soul!
6.23.1947 - 4.15.2015

Victor Valley to West Point

C.A. Henderson

Table of Contents

Chapter 1

The Back Story

Everyone has a story. The question of whether that story can change the life of those around them can be debated. However, no matter what our story is, there are always lessons to be learned. I believe that my story will enlighten, and perhaps inspire, someone else –someone like myself who perhaps had a dream their whole life but gave up on it; or someone that has a dream and needs encouragement to follow their dream. This book is dear to my heart, and I hope it helps at least one brave soul that has the audacity to persevere and endure on the road of their dreams to see it come to fruition. This is the story of my life.

YOU CAN BE SUCCESSFUL IN THIS HARD COLD WORLD WE CALL PLANET EARTH WITH FOCUS AND PERSEVERANCE.

So let's begin at the beginning. Sometime in the 1960's my mother and father met in San Bernardino, California. Both of them were offspring of sharecroppers that migrated from the Southern states of Louisiana and Mississippi, respectively. My dad was working at the local Happy Boy Car Wash in the city of San Bernardino and my mother was in school. My father, being three years older than my mother and much more street savvy was able to make a very great impression on her early on. My father and his younger brother moved to San Bernardino to live with his older sister after their mother passed away when he was 12 years old. His biological father was out of the picture and his stepfather, whom he got his last name from, was also not able to care for them. Always very industrious, my father was determined to learn how to fend for himself. So he dropped out of Junior High school in order to earn money to take care of the family. He didn't want his older sister to have to carry the family burden. He was able to provide for his family working hard jobs and hustling scrap metal. Eventually he was able to land a job with the County of San Bernardino, from which he later retired.

My mother was the daughter of a preacher and the second oldest child of her mother. Although she grew up poor, their father always provided for them. He too was very industrious and had even served in World War II. They lived in the "Valley" area of San Bernardino and later moved to the west side of San Bernardino. She and her older sister also helped take on the childcare and work around the house until her older sister passed away from heart complications in her youth. My father courted my mother; they fell in love and eventually my mother became pregnant with my oldest brother in 1966, the same year they were married. My mother was only sixteen when she had my brother and my father was 19. Despite their ages, my mother didn't allow it to deter her dreams of getting an excellent education. She was still able to obtain her high school diploma from San Bernardino High School. She later went on to graduate with her Bachelor of Arts from Cal State San Bernardino.

My mother and father were married for eighteen years. During that time they bore three more children: my older brother in April of 1972, my sister in November of 1977, and finally I was the last child born January 8th, 1979. From what I was told, I wasn't exactly a planned event. After my mother had my sister in November of 1977, she "accidentally" became pregnant with me six months later in 1978. She said her pregnancy with me was very stressful, partly because she was caring for another baby all the while. My mother told me that she was often worried, and sad, during her pregnancy with me. Nevertheless, when I arrived, my family was excited. I was the youngest child and boy, and we lived on the west side of San Bernardino in a neighborhood known as the California Gardens.

My memories as a child go back to 1982 when I was three years old. There were positive memories as well as unpleasant ones. Some of the positive memories I have relate to when my parents were still married and living together with the whole family on 17th street. My sister and I would watch my mother roll Dad's hair in rollers. Back then, in the early 1980s, my father had a long perm that my mother would press and roll. Those were the "Superfly" days in the Black community and if you had a long perm, you were seen as an elite black man. My sister and I would jump for joy when my father came home from work. He always wore cowboy boots, and would ask us to help him take off his boots whenever he got home. This had become a ritual for the both of us, and we still talk about it to this day. Back then my father seemed so big to us, although he only stood about 5` 3`` in height. We just loved our dad and felt he could do no wrong. I also remember going on countless fishing trips with my family where my dad and mother would pack up the truck and camper and we would head out to local fishing sites such as Salton Sea and Lake Elsinore. When you're a young man, there's nothing like going camping or fishing with your family, especially your father and older brothers.

I also remember my mother being very loving and always wanting to do fun things with us. At the time, my mother's family was a very close-knit family headed by my fearless grandmother, and I remember my mother bringing us to grandma's house for many visits.

My mother loved her father very much. Unfortunately, he passed away in 1980 when I was only about a year old. I never had a chance to have a conversation with my grandfather but only heard great things about him. Shortly before my grandfather passed away, my mother converted her faith from Baptist to Jehovah Witness. This surprised much of her family, especially her father. But she remained a Jehovah Witness and took on their way of life such as not celebrating birthdays and holidays. The entire family attended a Kingdom Hall of Jehovah's Witnesses at my mother's request.

My mother's side of the family remained close until all of the grandkids started graduating high school and continuing on to college. We would always go to my Grandmother's house and visit her. I remember her house being my favorite destination as a young kid. All the family gatherings and events were hosted at her small house on Pico street, near the projects in San Bernardino. She would make her famous potato salad, collard greens and banana cream pie. My grandmother was an avid Los Angeles Lakers and University of Southern California fan. The reason why she loved the Trojans of USC so much was because my uncle played football at USC from 1977 to 1981.

My uncle loved football and his senior year in high school he was one of the nation's top recruits. He was a stand out football player and track star at San Bernardino High School. His older brother was also a stand out track star at San Bernardino High School before he joined the Air Force. Under the guidance of my grandmother, we would root for USC every football season. I even remember going to the Coliseum to watch USC play as a small child. There was something about seeing my uncle's name in the media guides and all of his accolades such as the Fiesta Bowl Trophy, Tommy the Trojan Senior Award, 1978 National Championship ring and several other USC paraphernalia that won my heart at an early age. I knew then that I wanted to play football!

The Dream

Growing up, I completely loved the game of football. I watched it on television, looked at books and tried to play it whenever I got the chance. I always had a football with me at all times. I became one with my football. I would just walk around with it. I would run around the house with it. If I was somewhere with my football, I would petition different people to play catch with me. I would even play catch with myself if my sister didn't want to play catch with me. It was just that important.

My brothers were always stand out players as they grew up in San Bernardino playing for the South West Bears and other teams. They always planted the idea of playing football in my head as I grew older. They would always tell me that when I turned eight years old, I would be able to play football and run the ball. Until then, they just taught me different fundamentals of football such as how to tackle, catch, throw, and juke. My brothers would always play catch with me and teach me all kinds of things that involved football or just life in general.

As I grew up looking at all my brothers' and uncle's trophies, playing rack'em up with my cousins and dressing up in my brother's old football gear and helmets, I became more and more passionate about the game of football. I even started collecting football cards and any football I could get my hands on. We didn't usually have too much money back then, so most of my footballs came from the goodwill store, a place that was all too familiar to our family.

In 1983, my mother and father separated and we all moved out to the Waterman Gardens near Baseline Ave and Waterman Ave. Shortly after that, in 1984, my oldest brother graduated San Bernardino High School and went off to Tuskegee University. After living in the Waterman Gardens for a while my mother's tires were stolen and her car placed on bricks. With crime increasing, we moved in with my grandmother on Pico Street. This was the beginning of a poverty stricken, Section 8, welfare, and AFDC life. Despite the circumstances, **I had developed a passion that would later turn into an all out dream**.

We later left San Bernardino in 1985 to live in Fontana, where we moved to a town home on Citrus

Avenue. At this point, the family separated. My sister and I lived with my mother, while my two brothers lived with my dad. Sometimes my second oldest brother would move back and forth between my mom and dad's house. He did that on and off until he was seventeen, when he just started renting his own apartment. Living in Fontana back then was not easy. Fontana was well known for two things: their racist citizens and their football team. I remember little white kids calling us niggers at school.

I was able to get my first taste of football competition while we lived in Fontana through a parks and recreation league. At six years old, I came home excited and told my mother that I wanted to play flag football and I had the sign up sheet in my hand. Still too young to play tackle football, I was overjoyed when I heard about this opportunity to play at the park. My mother obliged and I was able to play at the park. I remember it only lasted a couple weeks, but it was the next best thing to tackle football and I loved it. They gave me a t-shirt, white with blue lettering that said: "Fontana Parks and Recreation Flag Football". I wore that shirt until I was about 12 years old. I was so proud of myself and my accomplishment.

Living in Section 8 housing was unpredictable. Sometimes our lease would unexpectedly end and we would have to move because the apartments we were renting dropped their Section 8 status. So we moved a lot. From Fontana, we moved to another Football City in the Inland Empire, Redlands, when I was in the 2nd grade. The reason we moved to Redlands is because my mother had recently been accepted to the University of Redlands after she graduated from San Bernardino Valley College. In Redlands, we lived in project style apartments that were just recently torn down in 2013. I remember we didn't have a refrigerator for months and the apartment was infested with roaches. Since we didn't have a refrigerator, we had an ice chest with supplies to make sandwiches. I can still remember the taste of those ham sandwiches on white bread to this day.

My sister and I were enrolled in Franklin Elementary School in Redlands, and we had to walk home from school every day to a day care center and wait for my mother to get out of class at the university. From Redlands we moved yet again to another famous football city in the Inland empire, Rialto, California. When we arrived in Rialto, my sister and I were enrolled in Bemis Elementary School. At Bemis, I finished second grade and completed third grade as well. Bemis was where I started to find out how good I was in football and also how much fun it was. Back then, we were not allowed to play tackle football in the elementary schools at recess. As a matter of fact, the classrooms were not even allowed to have footballs for recess. So what all the young boys would do is take soccer balls out to recess and simply hold them like footballs instead of dribble them with our feet. We would do this day in and day out until the teacher on duty would stop us. I remember it being so exciting to pick up that ball and run toward the goal, dipping, dodging, and juking kids as I would outrun them or break their tackles. It was the most exciting part of elementary school.

I entered the third grade the fall of 1987, and I was finally going to be eligible to play Rialto Pop Warner because I was eight years old and that was the age requirement. During this time in Rialto there was Junior All American and Pop Warner Football, ninth grade football at the Junior Highs and finally Eisenhower High School Football, which was the pride of the city. All the kids at my school played Pop Warner and the teams were all named after Native Americans such as the Renegades, Comanches, etc. I remember being so excited to get a sign up sheet for Rialto Pop Warner Football. This was it; I was finally going to be able to show out on the football field. All these years waiting to play tackle football has paid off. I couldn't wait to get home and show my mother the sign up sheet so we could fill it out, sign it, and immediately take it to the sign up table. This was going to be a dream come true.

By this time, my excitement was unbearable. I just couldn't wait to show my mother the football sign up form. So I got home and waited for my mother to get home. Excited as I could be I showed her the form and asked, "Momma can I play football for Pop Warner?" To my surprise, she looked at me with a straight face and said, "NO!" What? I couldn't believe this. All these years since I could remember I was waiting to turn eight years old so I could finally play football, the game of my dreams. Now the time was here, the sign ups were here, I was eight years old, and she's telling me no. I was absolutely heart broken as a little kid. My world was crushed. I tried everything I could think of to change her mind including asking my big brothers, my grandmother, my uncle, and my dad to talk to her. Nothing worked. She did not budge.

Being Jehovah Witness, my mother believed that she was doing the right thing by not letting me participate in competitive sports. She believed that bad association spoils useful habits, and since people of the world were bad association, then I shouldn't participate in any sports alongside them. I was crushed. I remember crying every year during football sign ups and football season. The only thing I wanted to do was play football on a team and have fun. I didn't understand her explanation for not letting me play.

Luckily my dream didn't die during this time of perseverance. Every year my love for football grew more and more. My dream to play became stronger and stronger every year. Everyone that knew who I was knew that I had football in my blood and there was a consistent passion in my body for the game. Football was me; I was football. Every year I begged to play and cried and pleaded, but it did not help my case. Everyone would ask me what team I played for, and I would have to tell them that I wasn't a part of a team because my mother would not let me play. I was continuously heartbroken every single year.

Henry Elementary

In the fourth grade my mother, sister and I moved again to another neighborhood in Rialto where we were finally able to rent a house from an older white couple. This neighborhood was known for the notorious apartment complex called the Glenwood Apartments and the neighboring apartment complex called the Vineyard Apartments that are still there to this day. Behind our house there were grapevines and wild jackrabbits that ran through the grapevines as fast as ever. I often found myself in those grapevines hunting rabbits. My oldest brother and my father would tell me stories about how they used to go rabbit hunting, and I always found enjoyment in those stories. I often found myself making weapons like slingshots and going back in those grapevines to hunt myself some rabbits. I would creep through those grapevines keeping my footing in the loose dirt and out of nowhere, a jackrabbit would pop out and take off running. I desperately would try and chase that rabbit to kill it with my slingshot, but to no avail. The rabbits were super fast and they knew the grapevines well. It also kept my mind off my disappointment of not being able to play football.

By this time I had already been transferred to Henry Elementary School to get a fresh start. At Bemis Elementary School, it didn't seem as if I was getting a fair chance, because I was often in trouble, and targeted by the teachers. My mother didn't want me to continue at that school so I was transferred. My sister, however, excelled at Bemis Elementary School. Straight A's was the absolute norm for her. She was very intelligent. I was intelligent as well, but just a little different. I always had credible scores, mostly A's and B's in elementary school, but those A's and B's came with referrals and suspensions until I got to Henry Elementary. Being at Henry, this would be the first time in years that my sister and I didn't attend the same school.

My transfer to Henry was a great move for me. I immediately fit into the school's system and did very well— never got in trouble, made lots of friends, excelled in PE class, and was popular with the kids at the school. We played tether ball, dodge ball, baseball and of course, soccer football. Just as the kids did at Bemis we would pick that soccer ball up like it was a football and have us a nice game going. This was the highlight of recess. There was nothing else exciting for me about school as football at recess. Henry elementary school also had an annual track meet for the whole school to participate in. Every year, I would train myself for this track meet, hoping to win myself some ribbons that I could show off to my brothers and the rest of my family. I still have those ribbons to this day.

Attending Henry Elementary school from the fourth grade through the sixth grade created some milestones in my life as well. I remember the exact day that I recognized and enjoyed looking at the butt of a girl when I was in the fourth grade. From that point on I was hooked. I had several crushes at Henry Elementary and a couple little girlfriends. I even managed to write a pretty well written letter to the girl who I noticed and she agreed to be my girlfriend, but her class went off track and I didn't see her for four weeks. Then, she was no longer interested. By the time I got to the sixth grade, I capped off a great three years at Henry Elementary by acquiring my first kiss. I was so excited, for I had only dreamed of such a thing before that. From my perspective, I was on my way up in this world.

At home, however, my sister and I were always fighting. If there was anything to argue about, we argued about it, and probably fought about it. I mean, we would go to blows or even worse, tear each other's belongings up at the drop of a dime. You see, we were latch key kids, and always had plenty of time on our hands before our mother got home from school to beat each other up or play dirty mean tricks on each other. We did all kinds of crazy things to one another such as me cutting the hair off all her dolls, taking a razor blade to her new shoes, and her pitching a shower scrubber at my head so hard that she shattered the glass shower door. One time it got so bad, my sister grew angry and threw all my socks and underwear in the bushes. I took revenge and committed to throw all of her socks and underwear in the bushes as well. Some of those same socks were still in those bushes years later when we moved out of that house.

Since we couldn't play with the neighborhood kids because they were not Jehovah Witnesses, my sister and I had to play with each other unless some kids from the Kingdom Hall were invited over, which was probably rare. As much as we fought, we still had love for each other. My sister supported my dream and passion for football by playing catch with me, and running routes while I threw her the ball and vice versa. When she got mad at me or just didn't feel like playing football with me, I would play catch by myself. Throwing the ball long and running underneath it diving for the ball in the front yard. I could throw myself a spiral pass and reach out, leave my feet and come down with it every time. Football was my dream, my love, and my passion. I continued to pursue it not even knowing if my hope to play would ever come to fruition. At this point in time, my mother was still strongly against me playing football or any other sport.

Since I was eight years old, I had been interested in football, basketball, and baseball. Unfortunately, my mother said no to me playing every one. I became disinterested in playing baseball and basketball competitively, but my love for football only grew. I brought my football with me wherever I went, even to church. I would run out the Kingdom Hall after the last prayer so I could go to the car and grab my football. There would be a sense of excitement and pride that came over me just from holding my football in my hands, tucked away like a running back. It was 1991, football was huge in Rialto at the time and I was heading into junior high school. Friday nights were on and popping during football season, especially if Eisenhower had a home game. It was the only high school in Rialto at the time and the football team was on college status. I was going to start seventh grade at Kolb Junior High School, and my next step would be Eisenhower. The excitement was in the air.

Chapter 2

The Grapevines

When I arrived at Kolb Junior High School it was a big adjustment for me academically. Socially, on the other hand, was smooth sailing. One major item that stood out like a sore thumb was that once you got to junior high school in the city of Rialto, unlike elementary school, all ethnicities hung around their own. Black people would only hang with other Black people; Whites with Whites, Hispanics with Hispanics, and so on. Kids that you were cool with in elementary school, that were different races, you didn't hang around in junior high school. You still may say hello in the halls or locker room, but you hung with your own on a regular basis. This wasn't a written rule, but it definitely was an unwritten one.

Kolb Junior High School, as well as the other junior high schools in Rialto, held seventh grade through ninth grade. My sister and I were back together again. She was in the ninth grade and she played in the band. As a seventh grader, I remember being a little intimidated by the older girls and I didn't quite have a plan developed for how to talk to them at that point. But all that changed when my brother put me on the spot one day at the house. We were outside in the front yard, probably playing catch with my football when this girl that went to my school walked by on the other side of the street. I just let her walk by and then I told my brother that I liked her. That was the wrong thing to do. He said in a disgusted voice, "If you like her, why doesn't she know that? You didn't tell her?" I said, "No." He said, "You'll never have a woman in your life because you're scared to talk to them and you have no game. You better get some game and stop being a punk." At that point I was embarrassed and mad at myself that my brother was disappointed in me.

That night I made up my mind that I would get me some game, and I would prove to myself and my big brother that I could indeed talk to the ladies. I was going to prove this by returning to school the next day and getting phone numbers from the finest girls in the school that I'd been lusting over all semester. From that moment, I went to school and pulled five phone numbers. I learned that day that all you have to do is talk for what you want and like, and be cool. That talk with my brother changed my life. The next day I went into action and gained some valuable confidence in myself.

In the classroom, I wasn't doing as well, but I did learn to type very well. I was used to getting great scores in elementary school, but for some reason that didn't transfer to junior high school. And not only that, I was always in the office with a class suspension or referral. Historically, I was always in gifted and talented classes throughout elementary, so I remained in those classes in junior high school. There were a lot of dudes in those classes that I didn't get a long with or just didn't like at all. And it didn't help that the teacher never sided with me. Every week a referral was being mailed to my home and I was trying to beat it home to intercept it. My English teacher, especially, really had it in for me. She would get on me about everything from my attitude, to how I wrote my letters in cursive. One day she actually wrote me a referral for not changing the way I wrote my letter "r" in a paper that I turned in. She was cold.

I didn't just have a hard time with my teachers, but I had to make sure I was tough around my peers as well. Protection and thinking ahead were on the minds of all the youngsters back then. Before school, cats would be slap boxing, free-style rapping, and dancing. In the early nineties, gangs, drugs and violence were at an all time high in the Inland Empire streets and it trickled down into the junior high schools since so many people's older brothers, uncles and even daddies were either gangsters, hustlers or criminals. This was the energy that was flowing through the school on a daily basis.

My school was one of two "Black" junior highs in the district since they changed the borderlines for all the junior high schools. The other so-called "Black" junior high school was Frisbie Junior High, and they were archrivals with Kolb. Kids from Kolb and Frisbie used to get into it just because of what school they went to and what neighborhood, gang or crew they belonged to. This rivalry with Frisbie was real and it even showed up on the football field. Every year, both schools would show up to either Frisbie or Kolb for the annual show down of the cities top two ninth grade teams. People still talk about that rivalry to this day. As a seventh grader and a football fanatic, I only dreamed of having a chance to play against Frisbie in this annual game.

One of the PE teachers that actually coached freshmen football at Eisenhower at the time was very enthused about football and all of the athletes that we had on campus. Some of these players were going to be Division I guys some day. This PE teacher took great pride in keeping the youngsters enthused about football and was constantly talking about us eventually playing for Eisenhower, a team that carried the city on their backs. Eventually he designed a flag football competition that changed the whole game on campus. This flag football, to me, was a dream come true. I would be able to compete against some high quality athletes at school, and my mother couldn't say no.

The flag football competition started out as a competition between teams in each period. After that competition was over the champions from each period would play another tournament for the bragging rights for the whole school. This was the ultimate football tournament, and I was very excited to be a part of it. All the athletes were either in third period PE with me or in sixth period PE. I've never seen so much talent in one junior high school since then. My team, in third period eventually won the tournament for third period even though we were considered the underdogs. We went on to beat the sixth period champions for bragging rights over the whole school. We won that game in the last seconds of the game after sixth period came back to take the lead. With just seconds left in the game, I threw a pass that was caught just inside the goal line to give us the lead and the trophy. We sang, "We are the Champions" all the way to the locker room as a surprised and very angry sixth period looked on. That was the height of my seventh grade experience.

During my seventh grade year at Kolb, our lease at the rental house 1099 West 2nd street expired with no chance of renewal. We were going to have to move again. Fortunately we were able to find an apartment just a couple blocks away from our old house to keep us in Rialto, and close to our friends and family. The unfortunate thing is that we were going to have to transfer schools. Although our new apartment was still in Rialto, it was within the boundaries for the Fontana Unified School District. These apartments were located near Merrill Avenue and Linden Avenue on the Southwest side of Rialto.

All the kids in our new neighborhood were being bussed to Alder Junior High School, and Fontana High School, which was one of the most popular high schools in the Inland Empire.

My sister was in the ninth grade and wanted to stay at Kolb to finish her ninth grade year with her friends and classmates. I wanted to stay at Kolb as well. We were determined to stay at our school and thought of a great way to do so. We talked our mother into not reporting to the school district that we had moved and to let us finish the year out at Kolb. She agreed, but we would have to find our own way to school and we could not rely on her to give us rides. We agreed to take the responsibility of getting to school and came up with a bright idea. Since our bus stop was simply about a mile from our new apartment, we would just get up earlier than usual and walk to our original bus stop and catch the bus to school like we had been doing all the while.

This easy and simple plan sounded better than it actually was. Although my sister and I were very enthused about our supreme plan, the bitter reality of it all came to smack us in the face. Although the walk was only about a mile from our apartments, the fact that it wasn't a straight shot was haunting us. The vast acres of grapevines were separating us from the bus stop. Unless we took the long way, walking all the way around the grapevines, we would have to walk through the soft sand of the grapevines every

27

morning to catch the bus. The walk seemed way shorter than it really was. This route was very long and forced us to get up earlier and walk faster to make it to the bus in order to get to school. After doing this a couple of days, we realized that it may be faster to cut through the grapevines instead of walking around them.

The very next day we started out on our new venture of cutting through the grapevines as a short cut to our bus stop. The grapevines, in the mornings, were very damp and the dew was still low. The soft sand was almost muddy and very loose, making it difficult to tread through. It was faster than walking around the grapevines, but very tedious and messy. My sister and I would be very frustrated walking through the grapevines in the mornings, usually arguing amongst each other because it was such a difficult walk. When it started raining and the dirt was more muddy than usual, we would tie plastic trash bags around our shoes so that our shoes would not get messed up. These trash bags would give our young minds hope, only to be let down when the bag ripped and exposed our shoes to the mud and endless dirt.

Despite the rain, dirt and long walks in the morning, sometimes before the sun had even come up, my sister and I persevered and fought the good fight. We stuck together and saw it through. This indeed was the road less traveled. We could have easily transferred schools and rode the bus with the neighborhood kids, but we made up our minds that we would stick with our plan and finish that school year. We walked to the bus stop, through those treacherous grapevines, rain, sleet or snow. Through Santa Ana winds we walked, jogged, and even ran if we were running late. We were determined to succeed.

The next school year my sister went to Eisenhower High School instead of Fontana High School via inter-district transfer. I was determined to stay at Kolb Junior High School despite the fact that I would no longer be able to ride the bus. During the summer we changed our address with the school district and they would not issue me a bus pass. Once again I would have to come up with an ingenious plan to get to school every day. That was when I used the bike my big brother gave me. It was a black dirt bike that I rode all around the city and loved dearly. I decided that I would ride my bike to school everyday. What I didn't realize, as a young eighth grader, was that the ride to Kolb from Merrill and Linden was at least a five-mile ride. But I was determined to make the trek.

Before school began, I road my bike to Kolb to figure out how long it would take me via bicycle to get to school every morning. The ride was just under an hour-long. So my plan was to get up at 5 am every morning, be out of the house by 6 am, and be to school by 7 am.

On paper, this plan was awesome, but then the bitter reality was introduced. The bike ride was uphill the whole way. I would be riding my bike from Merrill and Linden all the way up Cedar, which turned into Ayala pass Highland avenue, which is now the 210 Freeway, to Bohnert Street and Cactus. Not only was this ride uphill the whole way, but also when Cedar turned into Ayala Street, it turned into a two-lane street and there was no sidewalk. I had to ride my bike on the dirt shoulder with cars zooming past me the entire way. The Santa Ana winds seemed to be blowing in my face the whole way to school every morning, making it hard to peddle up hill. When the time changed, and it was still dark when I left home, half of my ride was in the dark. When the weather changed, I had to endure the rain, heavy dew, fog and serious winds to make it to school.

My last obstacle every day was crossing Highland Avenue. At the intersection where Highland met Ayala, there was no crosswalk, no stop signs or streetlights. I would have to wait, patiently, however long it took for a gap between cars big enough to run my bike across the street without being hit. And sometimes the wait was long because of early morning traffic in which people were on their way to work. Riding my bike to school that whole semester was one of the hardest things I've done in my life. It took dedication, discipline and determination.

Leaving home when it was still dark, riding up hill five miles against the wind sometimes an arms length from cars on a dirt surface. It would have made more sense to transfer schools. Especially since we upped and moved anyway and still had to transfer schools.

My mother had been looking to move back into a house closer to where we lived. She wanted to be in a single house and not bunched up with other tenants in an apartment complex. She found a place near Mill Street and Macy Street on the East side of Rialto. The school district for the neighborhood was Rialto.

She broke the news to my sister and I. For a whole semester my sister and I had been enduring the elements. I was riding my bike and she had been hustling rides from a friend of the family who also attended Eisenhower High School. We felt as if this was all in vain. After all this perseverance and determination we were going to move again and have to transfer schools anyway. The only upside was that my mother had found a mobile home that was spacious. My sister and I loved our new rooms and the big living room and dining room it had. There were other kids in the mobile home park as well. My sister would be transferring to the newly built Rialto High School that just opened in 1992. I would be transferring to Frisbie Junior High School on the East side of Rialto. We started our new schools in January of 1993.

When I arrived at Frisbie, I was welcomed with open arms. My PE teacher from Kolb had already phoned Frisbie's PE department and informed them that I would be showing up in the Spring. He told them that I was a good student and a stand out athlete. It made me feel good that I was taken care of when I arrived. While I attended, Frisbie had a reputation back then as the rowdy, thuggish, hood school. I had no idea what to expect when I arrived, but to my surprise, the vibes at Frisbie were great. I had a couple black teachers, one for English and the other for Social Studies. There were also plenty of Black girls in my classes.

I received a lot more play from the girls at Frisbie than I did when I was at Kolb. I guess all the weight lifting that I was doing had paid off. This would be the first time that a girl would ever ask me for my phone number before I could even ask her. This didn't go well with my mother's strict Jehovah's Witness beliefs, since I was not allowed to have girls call my home.

My PE class at Frisbie wasn't nearly as athletic as the class at Kolb. When it came to PE, I ended up running circles around my classmates, especially in football. Football was still my dream and holding strong in my heart. It was my last semester of eighth grade and ninth grade was fast approaching, bringing me close to my lifelong dream of playing high school football. I was ready to eventually be in the papers and play under the lights on Friday nights, but I didn't know how I was going to do it. My mother was still so against me following my dreams and pursuing my passion of playing football. Nonetheless, I didn't let it squash my excitement. When May came and my sister told me that Rialto High School was in spring practice, I missed the bus on purpose just to walk all the way down Eucalyptus to Rialto High School to watch the high school team practice. I was an eighth grader with a passion; I was so excited just to be there at their practice— my eyes big and wide. Football was brewing in my blood, and a miracle I needed to happen fast if I wanted to play football.

Around the same time as the Rialto football team was having their spring camp, the girls' basketball team was also having their spring tryouts. My sister had recently made some friends while at Rialto that semester and decided that she wanted to tryout for the basketball team. With my mother being so heavily against organized sports, she told my sister that it wasn't going to happen. My sister, begged and pleaded to let her try out for the basketball team. She even cried and went to the extremes that I went through every year since I was eight years old to convince my mother to let her play. My mother would not budge. Finally, my sister disregarded my mother's wishes and tried out in spite of her saying no. Not only did my sister try out for the team, but she also made the team. This changed our family for good.

My sister, having made the team, caused some type of reaction in my mother that I would be forever grateful of. After all these years of trying to convince my mother to let me play football and failing, she had finally changed her mind because my sister did the unthinkable and went out for the basketball team despite my mother's wishes. My mother told me "Well if she's playing basketball, I guess I'll let you play football." This was the shot heard around the world. My sister had single handedly changed my mother's mind by just going out for the basketball team. I was so excited I didn't know what to do. I was finally going to be able to suit up and play organized football for a high school. I was finally going to be able to show everyone what I could do on a real team. I could finally wear a real helmet, jersey, and pads; I was going to be a quarterback. My life lit up from that point forward. Everyday was surreal. I was so grateful and excited about my new venture as a Rialto Knight!

The rest of that semester was a blur. All I thought about was being able to start practicing with the team in the summer. On the last day of 8th grade, it was bitter sweet because I would finally be playing football for Rialto High School, but all my friends from Kolb were going to be playing for Eisenhower High School.

Still, I didn't let that distract me. I focused on playing football and getting ready for summer practice.

The Knights

When I weighed in for freshmen football in the summer of 1993 I was a slim 5 feet 7 inches tall and weighed 147 pounds. I had a vision of starting as the quarterback and I was determined to be a workhorse for the team. It had been a very long time coming. For years, ever since I could remember, my dream was to suit up on a real tackle football team and play. When my chance came, I had to make the most of it. All my dreams had been answered by being given the opportunity to play that football season.

The first day of practice was on a Monday and I was nervous and extremely excited to get on the field. It was also very hot, the beginning of July in the Inland Empire is always the likes of an oven due to the natural desert climate plus the smog that lay over the inland valley like a blanket, keeping all the heat in and increasing the temperature. I road my bike to practice along with my red igloo water canister filled with a couple ice trays from the freezer and tap water.

At practice there were a lot of the kids there

that I went to junior high school with and some kids that I hadn't seen or heard from since elementary school. The majority of the guys coming out for the football team were inexperienced and didn't know what they were getting themselves into. A few guys had played football as a kid and were part of the initiated and experienced. You could tell these guys from the other kids that looked nervous and out of place. Personally, I was uninitiated at that point, had never played football on a real team in my life, and had no idea what to expect other than the war stories that my older brothers had shared with me about their football days. I was full of emotions ranging from excited, to nervous, to joy. Some of the freshmen that were coming out for the team were smaller than me; a few were my size, and some bigger than me. I always compared myself to other kids my age cause I never wanted to be smaller than anyone else. So, lifting weights became my goal to improve myself physically.

When we had completed the normal warm up and stretching the coaches had finally got to the part that we'd all been waiting for. They wanted to know who wanted to play what position. This is like the biggest moment in football where you get to see your opposition. I loved the quarterback position and I was determined to play quarterback that season. I knew I was good –I had an arm, I could throw great passes and I had the agility to scramble and even get out of the pocket and run. My mind was made up, I was going to go out for quarterback and make it! There was only one thing, the other guy that was going out for quarterback had played quarterback for years in Pop Warner football; was a baseball pitcher, and he was already about six feet tall. Even so, I was determined to beat this guy for the starting spot. After all, the quarterback was the man! He was that guy, and Lord knows I wanted to be that guy, I had dreamt of the day for so many years. It was on.

As the days went by, my competition and I battled it out for rights to the starting quarterback position. We both were good athletes and could run the offense. But just like any other team, you can't have two starting quarterbacks so one of us had to win the job outright. It was a long hard fought battle, but I was named number two quarterback. He beat me out fair and square. He was taller, had a better arm, and had more experience playing the game. I tried my best, lost the battle, but I was not discouraged. I didn't have time to be discouraged, I had to use all the time I had now to find another position to play.

While I was battling it out for the QB position, the other great athletes on our team were taking all the other reputable skill positions. Luckily for me, we ran the Wing-T offense, which allows you to have multiple guys in the backfield. This is a great offense for teams that have a lot of talent at running back. Even though we ran the Wing-T, all the spots at running back were sewed up. The two wings were fast guys and we had a stud or two at the Fullback position. Basically, I was out of luck at running back. So one week away from the first game, I'm second string quarterback, and starting tight end, which any guy with quarterback or running back dreams, dares to be demoted to. All I could do is practice hard and wait for my opportunity to present itself. So that's what I did.

Then something unbelievable happened. One day before the first game our quarterback went down with a groin injury and I was told that I would start quarterback against Rim of the World the next day. I was both happy and nervous, but I was extremely nervous. I don't know if you've ever played back up to someone before, but it's the worst situation. When you're the back up guy, your mind is not on starting a game and leading your team to victory, it's usually on the position you've been demoted to or something else. But when the team needs you, the team needs you. I spent the whole night thinking about my chance to start at Rim of the World and how I was going to show the team and the coaches that I was the man. Not only was that my first ever football game, but I was the starting quarterback. Nervous didn't begin to explain it.

Game day came quickly. It was the first week of September, it was hot in the mountains and the air was thin. The excitement of football was everything that I had ever imagined. A lot was to be learned in that game, especially with my most memorable play. It was first down, and the coach called 28 Sweep. We got a descent pick up of yardage. Thirty-two trap was the next play called. I knew all the plays and we were moving the ball. In the Wing-T offense, every play sets up another play. The offense is pretty much run oriented, but there comes a time or two in every drive where it's time to pass off the boot or waggle motion that the quarterback repeatedly does every play.

The play came, "Eight waggle, eight waggle, ready, break." We set out for the line of scrimmage to run the play. Our wide receiver is ecstatic because this is his time to shine in the game. Everyone lines up excited and ready to take it to them. "Ready down, set, go," the play is off. I fake the trap, fake the sweep, I began to boot around for the waggle and I see the defensive end from Rim in my face, my receiver is wide open down field, but I do not see him. I turned into a running back and took off. It turned out to be a pretty good gain. And that ended up happening on every passing play of the game, which made the wide receiver furious at the end of the game.

We ended up beating Rim of the World 8-6 that day. So, what did the coaches, the team and I learned from all this? We all learned that I wasn't really a quarterback, but I could damn sure run the football. I was a running back, and a decent one at that. At that point, I thought of how my newly found talents would be used in the coming weeks of the football season. I didn't know at that time, but the team gave me a nickname "The Stallion," for my running efforts. The following week against the new school in Lake Elsinore, called Temescal Canyon High School, they hadn't worked me into the starting position at running back yet so I started at tight end. Some time in the second quarter they moved me to fullback and I never looked back. A couple games later they also started me at rover (strong safety) and I finished the season starting both ways. We ended the preseason 1-2 with the win over Rim of the World, and losses to Temescal Canyon and Arroyo High School of El Monte. The 1993 Freshmen Knights ended up 5-1-1 in league beating San Gorgonio, Barstow, San Bernardino, Colton, and a come back win over A.B. Miller. We had one loss to Pacific and a canceled game against Cajon High School.

My freshmen football season was one of the most important times of my life. It was truly a dream come true and a date with reality. It inspired me to **work harder and keep pursuing my dream** of playing football on Saturdays at a university. At the end of that football season, I was honored as the 1993 Rialto High School Freshmen Football Most Improved Player. This trophy, even though only "Most Improved," was highly coveted and one of my all time treasured awards. It served as the gateway to my passion and a beacon of light and hope for the years to come.

Move to Victorville

Since 1979 my mother had dedicated her life to the Jehovah Witness religion and having done so, attempted to raise all her children accordingly. My older brothers didn't get bashed over the head with the Jehovah's Witness religion as much as my sister and I did because when they were growing up, my mother and father still lived together. Since my dad was in the household, they were only exposed a little bit. They both chose to go in opposite directions of the faith. However, my sister and I were very young, and when my mother and father split up, we still had a lot of growing up to do. This was primetime to get raised very heavily in the Jehovah Witness faith.

I adopted the mindset of my brothers about the faith, and early on my sister adopted the mindset of my mother in regards to the religion. My view of the Jehovah Witness religion was one of only don'ts and not being allowed to do anything, and I hated being involved in it. We would go to Bible study on Tuesday, another meeting on Thursday, field service on Saturday, and then to the Sunday service. This was way too much for a young kid. Although I do remember some children that really bought into this lifestyle, the majority of kids were becoming rebellious once they hit their teens.

My rebellion started around eleven or twelve years of age. I hated going to the Kingdom Hall, I hated the majority of the people there, except for the young ladies. Most of all I hated going door to door in the neighborhood trying to bring people to Jehovah. My interest in the religion decreased to almost zero and I couldn't fake it anymore. Everyone that looked at me inside the Kingdom Hall could tell that I had gone astray and that I wasn't bothered by it, but my mother couldn't accept this reality.

She continued to force me to go to all of the Kingdom Hall meetings and events— even demanding me to attend field service on Saturdays. It got to the point where I would purposely wake up late, get dressed as slow as possible, and commit other shenanigans in order to purposely make us late or keep us from going altogether. This snowballed into an ongoing amount of tension and negative energy between my mother and I. She only wanted the best for her youngest son and if making me go to all these meetings and field service was going to spare my life, that's what it was going to be. I, on the other hand, looked at it as bogus and stupid; I wanted out. It was affecting me mentally and socially. I was what seemed to be a little depressed at times but wouldn't know what it was until years later. Socially, I was a boy who was forced to be an introvert because I was not allowed to associate with kids that weren't of the Jehovah Witness religion. This caused me to be somewhat of a loner and very secretive. Yet, I felt pulled in another direction because I wanted to socialize with other kids.

As my mother and I continued to argue about the Kingdom Hall more and more, it evolved into a confrontation about everything. We argued about my room, my chores, girls calling the house, etc. If you can name it, we probably argued about it and I believe that it all stemmed from me not wanting to conform to the ways and ideals of the church. Not to mention that I was in my early teens and at this age any young man was probably going to start poking his chest and questioning his mother's authority. That is surely what I was doing. I had grown taller than my mother who stands about five feet four inches. I was lifting weights more and more, watching my muscles develop and thought I knew everything, as all young men do. And it was getting worse as the days flew by. I was fourteen years old, and as my mother called it "smelling my own piss." It was time for a change.

One day as I walked into our mobile home that December, I heard my mother weeping. It turns out she was on the phone with my dad and had been talking to him for quite a long while about me. When I heard my mother crying I immediately grew curious as to what was going on. Did someone die? Was someone hurt? Listening in a while, I figured out that she was talking to my father and that they were discussing me. Then, she handed me the phone and said crying, "You're going to live with your dad!" Surprised, I took the phone and said "Hello." My father and I only talked for a few moments as my mother looked at me with tears in her eyes. He said that he would be down on Saturday night to come get me. That was three days away.

That night was so full of emotion and tears from my mom, my sister, and I. My mother was very sad because she had mixed emotions about the whole ordeal I would guess. Every mother, on one hand wants the best for her son and for him to be raised to be the best man he can be, but on the other hand, no mother wants to kick her own son out of the house. I'm guessing she felt like she was giving up on me. At first I resisted the idea of going to live with my father. This was mostly because I knew everything about all the area teams, and I knew that Victorville, the city my father lived in, and the Victor Valley football team was historically terrible. For the past few years the Victor Valley High School football team had either gone winless or maybe won a game. The year was 1993, and the team had just went 0-10 that season. I fought and yelled that I did not want to go live in Victorville to no avail. Life continued as usual the following day.

The next day I woke up, still surprised from the happenings of the previous night. I went to school and kept quiet, just pondering on what would be my sudden future. I knew that I had made a great impression on the coaches and that I had a good chance at becoming a star player at Rialto High School. I had grown to love Rialto High School, and I couldn't possibly leave. As that day progressed, I slowly started looking at the bright side. As a kid, I had begged my mother to let me go live with my dad. My dad was a strong willed disciplinarian, but he also was sort of liberal. He encouraged sports and found nothing wrong with giving girls our phone number. My dad could teach me several things that I needed to know about being a man and I loved going to visit him on the holidays. Why not go live with him permanently? And if Victor Valley High School was so bad in football, I thought that perhaps I would stand out there and become a star. My selfish desires for stardom and other reasoning started to change my mind about the situation.

By the end of that school day I had made up my mind that I was going to leave Rialto, California on Saturday, head out for Victorville to my new home with my dad and stepmom, and never look back. I didn't tell too many kids at school that I was leaving. I don't remember even telling my coaches –I just packed up and left silently. When my father picked me up that Saturday evening I said my teary eyed good byes to my sister and mother, and left.

When we arrived at my dad's house in Victorville, I immediately began making it into home.

My most prized possessions and accolades, which included my flag football trophy from 1986, pictures of my mother, sister and brother, and my 1993 Freshman Football Most Improved Player plaque. It was Christmas break and school didn't start until two weeks later on January 3rd, so I had time to just chill and get used to my new home and new reality.

Victor Valley to West Point

Chapter 3

Home of the Jackrabbits

Christmas break came and went, and the first day of the Spring semester was here. I was ready to find out what Victor Valley High School was all about. I had some idea about the football team from their reputation and I got a look at their program record while I was in the school office registering. They had zero wins and ten losses. That made me tense, and my expectations weren't good. On top of that, I was nervous that there wouldn't be any Black people there, especially girls. I was also uncomfortable with the thought of dating a white girl. Besides, I grew up in the 80s and 90s, the "Jungle Fever" era, where interracial dating was frowned upon. Nevertheless, there was no turning back now.

The bus stop was right on the corner of our street, at Cypress Ave and 11th Street. When I got to the bus stop, I noticed that there were some Black people in the neighborhood. I was pleasantly surprised.

I wasn't used to hanging out with the kids in the neighborhoods because historically, my mother wouldn't let my sister and I hang out with the neighborhood kids. Being Jehovah Witness, she only wanted us to associate with the Witness kids that were in our congregation. My dad, on the other hand, encouraged sports, and having friends no matter what church or religion they belonged to. The problem was that since I wasn't used to hanging out with other kids, I had become somewhat anti-social. I was never really a true introvert, but I had grown to be the type of person that did everything on my own. I didn't care to talk or get close to too many other people. This may also have been a product of moving around so much as a young kid. Every time we got close to someone it was time to move on again. I guess my sister and I just became conditioned to not allow ourselves to get caught up in the emotional stress of getting to know people or making good friends.

Now I was away from my Mother's house and it was time for a new beginning. This desire for a new beginning may have been the reason that I agreed to move away to Victorville. Victorville in January is usually sunny but very cold and the air is brisk. The morning air made my breath visible as I walked onto campus. I had my school schedule of classes and was excited to be placed in a couple honors classes but offended by my PE class. My PE class was ordinary PE and not sports PE. This was an absolute problem. I chose to go to the counselor's office to replace that PE class with a football class that same period.

Sports PE made lifting weights and working out with the team during the spring more feasible. I wanted to be bigger, faster, and stronger for the season. The counselor told me that freshmen weren't usually placed in sports PE, and I would need the head football coach to sign off on the request. I rushed to the head coach's office.

When I arrived at the fields, the coach was a big older guy with a crooked smile, resembling a cowboy. He also held the title of ASB director. He was a known name in Victorville who served several stints as head coach at Victor Valley. I told him that I had just transferred from Rialto High School and I needed to be in his football class sixth period. He looked at me and sized me up. He asked me a few questions about my positions, to build a little rapport with me. Then, surprisingly, he said "I won't be the head coach next year, but I'll sign off on this paper because you look like you're serious about football." Shocked, I said "OK." I thanked him and ran back to the counseling office to get my schedule changed.

At lunch, the first day of school, I was staying in my introverted comfort zone, not really talking to anyone. I was checking out the scene and deciding which girls I wanted to get to know until three guys approached me and started talking. The youngest one was also a freshmen and was doing most of the talking. Apparently he was from Long Beach, and had moved to Victorville a few years prior with his family.

His brother, who was standing right by him, was a senior and the other one was a sophomore. They wanted to know who I was, where I came from and why I was chilling by myself. So we talked the rest of lunch; I had just made some good friends. As much as you hear stories of people getting tested when they first arrive at a different school or new place, that wasn't the case with me. Everyone was cool and welcoming.

After lunch, I had one class before football sixth period. Football was my life, my dream, and just being in the class was major excitement to me. We played touch football at first under the supervision of the old head coach. It was fun and I was excited. I fielded the obvious questions that a new guy would field and started conversations with different people. It was a successful introduction to the class.

That day after school, as I approached my bus I saw something that instantly grabbed my attention. It was a girl of course. I was immediately attracted and wasted no time approaching her. I walked up to her, not knowing what to expect, and said hello. Embarrassed, she smiled and said hello back. I proceeded to get her name and she even gave me her phone number. Feeling like a champion, I said goodbye and proceeded to my bus. I was happy as hell that I got a phone number my first day of school and especially happy that I was in football sixth period.

That girl later became my first girlfriend. I was 15 years old. The funny thing about it is that we wrote letters for a couple days then never talked to each other again until we were probably sophomores. It didn't last long, which is typical of kids and high school.

Ray Moore Stadium

Ever since I was young, I had this thing for football fields, the gridiron. Whenever I saw one I would get excited. If I had the privilege to walk or run on a football field, I was even more excited. When I first set foot on Victor Valley's campus, I walked to the football stadium, right through the gates and onto the field. I looked at the grass and the stadium, at the scoreboard and there it said, "Ray Moore Stadium." Ray Moore Stadium is home of the Jackrabbits of Victor Valley High School and to this day I can't walk into that stadium without getting goose bumps.

I was excited by the fact that Victor Valley High School had its own football field and stadium. The school that I transferred from, Rialto High School, didn't have a stadium or lights. They had to play every home game away, usually at Eisenhower High School. Now I was at a school with a stadium, lights, and a nice field that the groundsmen took pride in. It was a privilege for me to be there.

Our new head coach, a middle aged Hispanic man with a sharp eye and the attitude of a disciplinarian introduced himself to the team. He immediately ran down his background and that he had been successful in Riverside at Norte Vista High School by turning their program from mediocre to playoff bound. He would have a lot of work to do at Victor Valley, coming off a zero win season. He did express great expectations while looking at the returning starters. He also saw some hopeful freshmen that would be moving up from the freshmen level as sophomores the next season such as myself, our linebacker, tight end, and corner. He coined the phrase: "Refuse to Lose" as our team motto for the 1994 season. We had a lot of work to do. It was time to begin.

By this time it was mid January and every school in the nation was beginning their Spring weight training. In high school football there are three seasons: Pre-season, Season and Post-season. The Pre-season lasts from January to August. The Season lasts from September to November. And the Post-season lasts from December to January. At the time, we were getting ready to start our pre-season training. Our coach brought in this proven program called Bigger Stronger Faster. His goal was to implement this weight lifting and speed program at Victor Valley and it was supposed to be the X-factor in our performance. From the beginning I was sold by the head coach. He had me convinced that we could do it.

We immediately began our program, which consisted of lifting weights on Mondays, Wednesdays and Fridays, and running and calisthenics on Tuesdays and Thursdays. The weight lifting consisted of core lifts that included squats, cleans, dead lifts, and bench press. The running and calisthenics included all kinds of jumps, jump rope, stadiums, hills and wind sprints. Even though this was hard work, it was working wonders for my body, spirit and mind. I was absolutely thrilled over lifting weights, seeing my muscles develop and getting recognizably bigger and stronger. A great weight program is very valuable to the confidence of young men, athletes especially. I am a living example of this. Our coach pushed and pushed and pushed us. Some of the lazy ones could not take his aggressive demeanor and no nonsense attitude. Most of the lazy people quit or were kicked off the team. The strong, however, pressed on throughout the spring.

We continued to get stronger even through the track season when our coach encouraged us to be a part of the track team, but most of my buddies didn't want to run track. I was encouraged to run track by my uncles, who were both track stars, and my brothers. So I lifted weights at football practice and then went to track practice. A spirited Black man who now rests in peace headed the track team. I have to say that during my years at Victor Valley, my track coach was very helpful and believed in me. Track ended in May, and by the time May came I had put on several pounds on my bench press, squat, clean and dead lift. I was still a freshmen, but I looked like an upper-classmen.

I continued to be self-motivated. I wanted to be big, strong, fast and I wanted to skip Junior Varsity and start on the Varsity football team as a sophomore. That will and desire to start as a sophomore and suit up in Ray Moore Stadium, "Home of the Jackrabbits," was what kept me going that year. At the very same time all this was happening, I was still trying to adjust to living with my father and my stepmom, whom I had never lived with before outside of visiting. This was a big challenge for all of us, and at times discouraging, but they always encouraged me to do well in school and sports. I was kept afloat by my life dream of football.

When school ends and summer begins, sports training begins to increase. In the 1990s, Victor Valley High School always went on summer break around the second week of June. From June until August the summer workouts have to be endured despite the High Desert's infamous dry heat. Daytime temperatures in the High Desert area of California can reach into the 100s. Only the strong survive the summer workouts. Our coach always preached mental strength, he was a firm believer in Vince

Lombardi's coaching philosophy in which mindset and mental strength are pillars. To toughen us up mentally and challenge the weak, our coach decided that our summer workouts would start at 6 a.m., and we would have to be there by 5:30 a.m. This, he said, was a two edged sword. We could successfully beat the heat of the High Desert by working out early, as well as weed out the weak minded individuals that were not dedicated enough to be there at six in the morning.

The summer was filled with passing league tournaments where we threw the ball against other high schools in a seven-on-seven format. This was where the players got evaluated by their coaches, and sometimes even scouts. We even road tripped to Las Vegas, Nevada for a major passing league tournament that they host every year. That was the same weekend my second oldest brother graduated from the University of California, Riverside as the first African-American to complete a Chemical Engineering degree. Unfortunately, I had to miss his prestigious graduation.

August was fast approaching and due to the hard work and dedication that we put in, my partner that played corner and I, were looking at starting in the secondary. He was at corner, and I was at free safety. If we kept it up, we would be starting as sophomores for Victor Valley and it was very likely. Ever since my freshman season at Rialto High, I had set a goal to start as a sophomore on varsity. Working hard toward my goal was finally paying off.

Sophomore Season 1994

August approached before we knew it. It was 1994— my sophomore season of football. The first game against Quartz Hill High School was all we talked about as a team. Before we could think so far ahead, we had to conquer hell week in the Victor Valley heat. Hell week used to be a time when a football team practiced two or three times per day for a period of one or two weeks right before school started. Hell week consisted of a morning practice and an evening practice and usually included a session in the weight room as well. You get the idea of why this week was labeled as hell week.

I went into hell week competing for the starting job as free safety. I was confident that I could make this happen but there was only one thing that could stop me. There was a senior free safety that paid his dues in the program and was supposed to be next in line as the starting guy. Up until now, we had shared all the reps in the spring and summer workouts. With just a few short weeks to go until the season began, I was shown some favor, but we didn't know who was going to take the job. My coach wanted to go two platoon that season, in which there was an offensive team and a defensive team, so my hopes of playing running back that season were set aside. All I had to concentrate on was playing free safety and winning this starting job. I did the best I possibly could, running track, and successfully completing the spring and summer workouts to prepare my body for this adventure. Then, it was show time.

Our coach was a disciplinarian and a true believer in being a well-conditioned team, so our hell week was fierce. I had worked out all spring and summer with the varsity team and I was going to have to show if I could hold my own in pads on a varsity level. This was the real test. Through spring and summer camps, one may be able to hide their timidity or fears running around in shorts and a t-shirt. When this time of year came around, the pads either bring the man or the fear out of you, and the coaches are able to assess how well you'll hold up in a game of hitting, blocking, and tackling.

It was tradition at Victor Valley, as well as other schools, to start the first day of pads off with a few good hitting and tackling drills to assess those who were cut out for the football team. The first day of pads was a frenzy— whistles blowing, coaches and players cussing, and that good old sound of pads colliding. This was football.

The 1994 Victor Valley Jackrabbit's Hell week was full of competition and bragging rights. This culture trickled down from the assistant coaches, namely the running back coach and my defensive back coach. The running back coach played for Victor Valley in the late 1980s, and my defensive back coach was a crazy Latino man that appeared to have no fear. When these two coaches became a rivalry, the running backs and defensive backs adopted that same rivalry and it appeared to be war every day at practice. The down side to this rivalry was that the running backs seemed to be a lot bigger and stronger than us defensive backs.

I was probably the biggest defensive back at the time and I weighed in at 5ft 10 inches, 163 pounds that season. My good friend that played corner probably weighed a few pounds less. These running backs, one of which turned out to be one of the best in San Bernardino County that season, were 180 pounds and up and very powerful. Hell week, for me was a humbling experience. I took my lumps as well as put in a little work myself on some other people. I was young, so for the most part I was learning as much as I could as fast as I could in preparation for my sophomore debut against Quartz Hill High School. I was humble with pride as the season approached.

The first day of school always ended Hell week and the first game was always that Friday night. In 1994, I played my first varsity football game for Victor Valley High School against Quartz Hill High

School, located near Lancaster, California. I was starting free safety. The feeling was kind of surreal that night— like I was playing in a dream or in a movie. I did well for a rookie, but no one really did too well overall as we lost that game 52-31. Quartz Hill had an awesome quarterback who could run and throw the ball. I remember him running for a touchdown and suddenly breaking into the high step as he approached the end zone. It was a very intense game, but Victor couldn't pull it off that night. That loss, however, didn't diminish my excitement in getting to play on the varsity team.

Next up was the coveted Axe Game against Desert rival Barstow High School. It had been several years, since 1989, that Victor Valley had possession of the Axe, and we were on a mission to recover the Axe and bring it home where it should be. Being new to the area, I had to get a crash course on the rivalry between Victor Valley and Barstow, which began in 1932. This rivalry always brought a packed house whether it was played at Victor Valley or Barstow High. The winner of the game would always color the blade of the axe their respective school colors. This game was a big deal as it was the second longest running high school rivalry in California.

At this time, Barstow High School was known for their two stand out players. One played quarterback and the other fullback. Both highly recruited and had been all league honorees for the

San Andreas League the previous year. This would be their senior year and we were game planning to stop their show. The quarterback was a roll-out quarterback who would always tuck it and run if no one was open, but he could also get the deep ball off if the opportunity presented itself. Our plan was to roll the secondary to the side that the quarterback rolled out to. This would leave the free safety to play the alley and not allow the quarterback to kill us on the run, but still have all zones defended.

I remember one occasion when the quarterback sprinted out to my right, we rolled our coverage and I came quickly to the alley. He sprinted to the sidelines as I chased him. I knew I had him and prepared to make the tackle, little did I know that his receiver had circled back to take me out of the equation. I pursued, and within a split second he knocked the shit out of me. The crowd roared as I lay there for a second, eyes watery and nose filled with snot. I jumped up with tears in my eyes, but acted like it didn't fade me. I looked up into the northwest side of the stands where my family usually sat to see their reaction. Barstow went on to beat us 40-0 in the Axe game. My young eyes had once again been opened to the realities of varsity football.

After the Barstow game, we won a few more games and lost a few. Finally, it was time for the biggest of all rivalries in the High Desert— the Bell Game! The Axe game was the oldest rivalry that

Victor Valley High School competed in, but the Bell Game was the most anticipated, competitive rivalry in the High Desert and ranked very high among all rivalries in the entire state of California. The Bell Game started in 1969, in which Victor Valley and Apple Valley High School competed for an old train station bell. The winner of this gridiron battle held the bell until the next game was played. No matter how well or how awful either of the two teams were performing in any particular season, The Bell Game never lost its rank or excitement. I couldn't wait to be initiated into this small class of young men playing in the Bell Game.

I was not ignorant to the importance of rivalries and the impact they had on the whole city, the schools, and the youth football teams. I was ready to take on the challenge influenced by the passion of the senior players who, for a couple seasons in a row, had come home defeated. The seniors were very intense the whole week leading up to the game. Finally, Friday came after a long week of practice and elevated emotions. School seemed to fly by on game days and at last we were in pre-game doing our warm up drills. Within a blink of the eye, the National Anthem was playing and it was time for us to get on the field. Crosstown tensions and animosity were all brought to the table. The stands roared with more than 5,000 people. Photographers from the High Desert Daily Press and other newspapers flashed photographs and roamed the sidelines. The coaches were yelling and strategizing, and between plays, "Teen Spirit" and "We Will Rock You" were some of the songs used to heighten the adrenaline.

After four quarters of bone crushing hits, speedy runs, and fantastic passes we were tied at 21-21. When the 4th quarter gun blew the crowd was off the hook. Both sides were screaming "Ding dong, ding dong." Apple Valley cheerleaders were ringing the bell non-stop. The game and bell could be anyone's at that point. Then, we went into overtime, when each team gets four downs from twenty yards out of the end zone. Whoever has the most points at the end of the round wins the game. Apple Valley won the toss, and went first.

Apple Valley's sidelines and fans were going crazy as they went three downs without scoring. They huddled up and waited for the decision from their coach, but he didn't send in the kicking team. Apple Valley was about to line up and try to stick it in the end zone. The quarterback called the play and they broke the huddle. Apple Valley lined up in a familiar formation. We checked to our appropriate defense and awaited the snap. Ready. Set. Hut. The center snapped the ball, the quarterback handed off to his right, our defensive left, which was the side I was on. Apple Valley's running back ran the ball from about three yards out sweeping around to my side. There he dove past me into the end zone. The Apple

Valley crowd went hysterical. He barely made it in, but he was in nevertheless. Touchdown! Apple Valley went for the 1-point conversion, made it, and was up 28-21. Then, it was our turn.

Our offense took the field. The defense stood there watching from the sidelines, angry about the previous play. First and ten at the twenty. Coach sent the receiver in with the play; our strong running back ran just inside the ten. The crowd was standing on their feet. First down and goal. When it came time for the fourth down and a couple yards, down by a touchdown, and everything on the line, Coach sent in the play. The quarterback called the huddle: *"Sweep right on one, sweep right on one, ready, break."* This was it; everything was on the line and everything to lose. Our 1994 team had a great running back, one of the best in the County of San Bernardino, and we were going to get on his shoulders to pull us through. "Set, go," the quarterback yelled as he received the snap and handed off right to the running back. He bounced off several defenders and scored. Touchdown!

Our sidelines went wild, not realizing that we were still losing the game. It was now 28-27. Did we want to tie the game or go for the win? Without hesitating, our coach put up two fingers. We were going for the win! Again, the offense called the play, "Set, go!" The quarterback again handed the ball off to the All County Running back. The call was a dive play but the middle was full of Apple Valley defenders. The running back bounced to the right and plowed forward as he was hit once, twice, and three times. Feet still moving, body still going forward, he landed into the end zone. The whistle blew. The referee signaled that he made it in. Our student body jumped the gates of the bleachers and poured onto the football field; the senior players and cheerleaders immediately went and captured The Bell. They started ringing it and ringing it, taunting the Apple Valley players who looked disgusted with defeat. We won the game. It was The 1994 Bell Game, my first Bell Game, and a game that would go down in history as one of the most exciting Bell Games to have ever been played.

The rest of our Citrus Belt League play was not so fortunate, losing to Redlands High school, Eisenhower High School (in my home city of Rialto), Fontana High School and even Hesperia High School, who had a shifty sophomore running back, in a 30 degree, frozen battle for fourth place in league and a chance at an at-large playoff birth. We finished the season 4-6, 1-4 in league play. Our only league win coming in the "Battle of the Bell." We had a couple All Citrus Belt League selections at the close of the season and as a sophomore I was included as a 1994 2nd Team All Citrus Belt League pick along with my good friend who played corner. At the awards banquet I was fortunate enough to earn the 1994 Victor Valley High School Football "Most Improved " trophy. As a team we fell short of some goals, but personally I was excited for the next season and ready to start working hard in anticipation of it.

1995

Enter the year 1995. It was a memorable year for both good and bad reasons. The regular routine of classes, pre-season football and track and field were going as planned, until I received notice that my mother developed breast cancer and would be undergoing surgery to remove her left breast. I remember writing things like "I love you Mom," and "Mom" on my track spikes to serve as a dedication to her speedy recovery. One Saturday our track team was at the Inland Empire Track Championships at the University of California, Riverside in which my oldest brother picked me up early from the track meet so that we could go to Kaiser Hospital of Fontana to visit my mother after her surgery. I remember it like it was yesterday because on my last triple jump I rolled my ankle and landed head first into the pit. When I arrived at the hospital to see my mother, I was limping and in lots of pain. I was so very happy to see that she had made it through surgery with no more signs of cancer. This would be one of her three battles with cancer.

The upside in the midst of my mother's cancer battle was all the accolades and accomplishments that my sister had received. She was designated salutatorian of the Class of 1995 at Rialto High School, accepted into many schools, including MIT, Stanford, and UC Davis, and awarded various scholarships for her academic excellence. She decided on attending Stanford University on an academic scholarship, following in the footsteps of our uncle who was a Stanford graduate. The whole family was so proud of her.

My sister's accomplishments inspired me to continue to improve and make a name for myself on the gridiron. That spring, I started getting some recruiting mail from schools such as Colorado and different military academies. I was going into my junior year, getting bigger, and I showed an increase of speed in track. I was strictly focused on going out and opening the eyes of scouts this coming season. My good buddy, who was going into his senior year, was being heavily recruited. We all admired that and wanted the same for ourselves our senior year. My plan was to show off on the field, so the scouts that were coming to see him, would notice me as well, and come back for me my senior year. My dream and goal of playing Division I football was clear and my plan was coming together.

Another milestone was happening in my life during this year as well— I was determined to lose my virginity. Most of the teenage boys I knew were trying to be initiated into the Fraternity of Sex. I had always had girls, but never moved on to the next step. Then, I met this certain pretty young lady at school. I remember that she always wore short shorts to school and had a curvy-shaped body, which made those short shorts stand out even more and get her more attention from boys. I would always flirt with her but she paid no attention for the longest time. Finally, one day she gave me her number and I began calling her in the evenings, and writing her letters during the day at school.

She grew fond of me. My desires, and my hormones, grew more fond of her by the minute, and I wanted to seal the deal with her as quickly as possible. I could tell that she was perhaps a little more experienced than I was at the time. When I asked her about it, she suggested we wait until spring break when we would have more time during the day to hang out. Spring break arrived and we set up a day to hang out at a time that didn't interrupt my track practice. She gave me directions to her house, which was in walking distance from mine. I remember it being a very hot day. I jumped in the shower, nervous and excited about what was supposed to happen. This event is a milestone in any young man's life. I brushed my teeth and sprayed on some of my cheap cologne. I grabbed the one condom that I received from a friend and took off walking to her house in the heat of the Victorville day. When I got to her house I rang the doorbell and she answered, calm as usual, unlike myself.

When I went into the house I was surprised to see that her kitchen had ants, which through me off a little, I must admit. Yet I was not distracted from the original mission. We conversed for a while, and then she invited me upstairs to her room. This is where it all happened. She even put the condom on for me. It was over in T-minus 30 seconds. I was initiated, yet very embarrassed. No one told me that my first time was going to be over before it started. I had only heard talks before of people having sex for hours, and this was not the case for me. I was very confused. I left her house feeling horrible and completely embarrassed. When I saw her at school I was expecting it to be awkward and for her to make fun of me. As I grew older, I always wished I could have that moment back, a do-over.

The spring and summer of 1995 are vague in my memory bank. All I remember is lifting a lot of weights and running a lot of hills in preparation for our upcoming season. Everyone was getting very strong and gaining muscle mass. I had put on 13 pounds of muscle and weighed 176 pounds. I had finally reached Division I weight. Most of our team my sophomore year, were juniors, so we were looking forward to an awesome team for the '95 season. Everyone was experienced on the Varsity level in addition to some new sophomores that would be able to help out the team as well. Everything was on the upside, until we experienced a couple of unfortunate events.

The first blow was when three of our players were kicked off the team in the spring, including our All County running back. We were depending on him that season, but now we had to move on without him. Our coach looked for a way to utilize our team speed and agility, so he implemented the Wing-T offense into our practices. Expectations were very high for our team since the school had went from 0-10 in 1993 to 4-6 in 1994. We expected to do way better than .500 for the 1995 season.

Going into that '95 season hopes were very high and the excitement of the team was high as well. We were predicting playoffs and a Citrus Belt League title. We would have to beat all three of the schools down the hill to pull off a league championship. Eisenhower High School of Rialto, Fontana High School and Redlands High School were usually the schools that took 1st, 2nd, and 3rd place in our league. My school, Victor Valley High School, Apple Valley High School, and Hesperia High School usually played for a very intense and ruthless 4th, 5th, and 6th place, never seeing the playoffs. Hesperia High School actually beat Redlands High School in 1993 to make it to the first round of the CIF playoffs but to no avail. This year was going to be different. We planned on taking out those powerhouses and sweep the desert schools to get a shot at the CIF Division I playoffs.

After the previous season, the coaching staff switched me to strong safety. Recruiters were at our practices all through the summer and the newspapers were giving us positive predictions. This was a big deal as Victor Valley usually wasn't ever talked about in the preseason reports and just expected to do bad or worse than every other school. That year we received our preseason props and everyone was talking about the great chance we had with the athletes returning to our team. Finally, it was our time to shine.

We started out the 1995 season with a close win over Highland High School of Palmdale, California. We showed up to this game with our all white uniforms on, thinking we were going to take it to these guys and before we knew it, we were in a dogfight. We ran safety blitzes and really put the pressure on their quarterback. We fought hard and never gave up. In the end we came out victorious and went back to Victorville with a "W" for the record books. We were now 1-0 and the newspapers were showing us love on Saturday morning. Back then, high school football players lived for Saturday mornings. Saturday morning was the time where you bought the local newspaper with a hope to see your team, better yet your face, on the cover of the newspaper or the front page of the sports section. This was every boy's dream in the mid 1990s. I remember fantasizing about having my picture in the paper, and at the very least, my name in the paper giving me my props for how I played the previous night. That was motivation to work harder in the weight room, on the practice field, and in the games.

Our next battle would be the 1995 renewal of the "Battle of the Axe" against Barstow High School. The previous year, 1994, they whooped us with a score of 40-0. But this year, their stand out QB/DB and LB/RB were off playing on Saturday mornings at the University of Idaho. We felt like we had a solid chance of going up to Barstow and putting hands on them for four complete quarters, and bringing back our precious axe that we so greatly cherished and adored. It was a long bus ride to Barstow, especially under the anxious conditions that existed and all the crosstown rivalry that summed up this game. After all the pre-game speeches and getting cussed out by our position coach we were set to take the field. The moment of truth.

Barstow, located about an hour Northeast of Victorville, on Highway 15 towards Las Vegas, was an old country town full of proud people and hard-hitting football players. They would never just let you walk in and push them around without a fight. That night we went in with the intention to tear them to shreds and that's how we started off the game. We went up early in the first quarter by a lead of 6-0. A couple series later, Barstow responded with a score of their own and got up by a score of 7-6. We fought and they fought back. At halftime, Barstow was up by a score of 14-12. They also had a do or die running back, #22, that held nothing back. We hit this guy and he hit us back, we hit him more and he just kept coming back for more.

This was one of the toughest Axe Games that I had ever played. When the dust settled, Barstow High School came out victorious. They edged out the game 20-12, which was one of the closest Axe Games to that date. They ran over to the coveted axe, raised it high in the air and celebrated in our faces. As a team we experienced disgust and hate. The seniors especially were hurt, for this was their last chance as Jackrabbits to bring home The Axe. Myself and the other members of the junior class vowed that we would bring back that axe next season.

After a tough loss to our cross-town rival Barstow High School, we went back to the drawing board and attempted to get better and pull things together. There was still hope and we were trained to be fighters and mentally tough. Our coach always preached mental toughness, which has always stayed in the back of my mind throughout life, even after my football days extinguished. We set out the next week on a mission to pull off another victory against Montclair High School. After we beat Montclair High School, the season took a drastic turn for the worse— we lost our final two pre-season games. Victor Valley ended the pre-season with a 2-3 record. There was still hope and we believed, but we had to get through the infamous Bell Game. This year was a little different. In 1994 we won the game on the field, but due to an ineligible player, the league made us forfeit all our games and give the bell back to Apple Valley. What we agreed to do, since the game was won on the field by us, was put the bell back in Apple Valley's possession painted a neutral color. It was painted an off white color, with the words "Limbo" on the front. The coveted bell would normally be painted in the color of the team that won the previous year. We won the previous year on the field, but had to forfeit the game. Therefore we were instructed to give the bell back. But since the Apple Valley team didn't win on the field, they agreed to hold the bell, but they declined on the opportunity to paint it in their colors. They painted the word "Limbo" on the bell because it was indeed, in limbo, having no real owner.

The Saturday before game week all types of scouts were calling letting the coaches know they would be on the sidelines. It was a huge deal. This year we would be playing in Apple Valley's Newton T. Bass Stadium, which was an ultimate joy to play in. Even though we hated Apple Valley, we loved their field. It was cut out of a hill. As you walked up to the stadium from the parking lot, you could see how they dug the stadium out and it sat very low below the stands. Once you got into the playing field, you could hear the voices, cheers, and shouts echoing throughout the stadium like it was an NFL stadium.

The whole setting brought chills to your arms and made your eyes open wide. During pre-game, as the crowd began to fill in the stadium, it started to feel more and more like it was a major college football game or perhaps a professional football game. Ten football scouts were on our sidelines watching us warm up. Probably about five different schools were represented as well to see who was worthy of playing on Saturdays. Apple Valley came out of the locker room in their Sun Devil orange jerseys with white pants. We road tripped in our white on white uniforms with the Kelley green helmets, game ready, war ready, and 'swagged' out.

Going into this Bell Game I was really excited and felt a lot of pressure because I was assigned to guard Apple Valley's standout junior wide receiver the entire game one on one. Wherever he went, I went. This 6'2'', 190-pound wide receiver had been tearing up teams over the course of the season. All week during practice I prepared for the challenge of covering him during the game, and I was confident going in. It was time to put everything on the table for the biggest game of the year.

The National Anthem played and ended. The usual chill bumps that I got when the National Anthem played persisted and I knew it was time. The kick was off and the game had begun. The first play Apple Valley had from scrimmage was a test for me. I was playing man to man, inside shade to take away any inside routes that the big receiver tried. On the snap, he ran an inside slant. I was on his hip running with him when the ball came. I wrapped with my right arm and tried to bat the ball out with my left. He caught the ball despite my efforts. We were having our own battle within the battle every single play. Whether he was going out for a pass route, or he was trying to block me on a run play, the intensity was consistent throughout the whole game. Both of us gave our all in an effort to push our team over the edge of victory. I won some of the battles; he won some of the battles. It was a fair and entertaining match up for the crowd to watch.

Right before halftime the momentum shifted a bit. The Apple Valley sidelines and crowd was beginning to get loud and proud. Their junior wide receiver ran out of the huddle and lined up far to my left, right near his own sidelines. He had a look in his eye that seemed to be excitement. Wide receivers always look excited when they know they are getting the ball. Most defensive backs know that if a wide receiver lines up wide he's doing one of two things: going for the deep ball or running a slant. I was ready for the challenge. My chilly breath was flowing out of my helmet; the brisk Apple Valley breeze was cold on my hot arms. This would be the moment of truth and we both knew it. The scouts were here, the fans were here, we were out there on an island all by ourselves and this was it.

He stepped quick inside, I matched him with a step the same direction and punched him in the chest with bump and run technique, he immediately switched directions and started up the sidelines. I was on his hip, and without even having to look back I knew that the ball would be coming shortly because he was the quarterback's favorite target. I looked him in his eyes as we sprinted tirelessly, full speed down Apple Valley's sideline. It was just he and I and finally, the ball. Since the ball was in the air, it was then time to play defense. I looked back for the ball sprinting down the sidelines. I turned to put myself in position, he gathered himself and got ready for the ball. I tripped over my feet and fell. The ball dropped into his hands, he caught it and backpedaled into the end zone victorious.

The Apple Valley sidelines and crowd went into a huge frenzy. The moment of truth was over. He beat me on a deep ball. I picked myself up off the ground and looked into the eyes of my pissed off defense. I had let them down in the biggest game of the year, and for some of us, the biggest game of our lives. The feeling of anger and disappointment ran through my veins for a few minutes, which seemed like an eternity. In life, you win some, and you lose some. That day, we lost and Apple Valley kept the bell.

Apple Valley pulled off a convincing win by a score of 32-21, and when the final gun sounded, they captured the bell from its lonely spot in the back of the home end zone. There's nothing more irritating than hearing the bell ringing when it's not your team making it ring. This was one, like all the rest of the Bell Games, I would never forget. The next day in the Saturday morning films the joke was on me: "I got beat deep by a white boy." In the Black man's inner circle this was the worst thing that could happen in a game. I took the jokes with pride, however, because I still had one more Bell Game to play.

This 1995 season was a disappointment. We lost every other game of the season except a convincing win over Hesperia High School, our other rival, by a score of 30-0. This was the game where I had my first concussion. I was playing fullback, and the call was 32-Trap. I went up the middle as the play was designed, but bounced outside because the middle was piled up. As I headed towards the sideline a Hesperia defender attempted to tackle me. My signature move while carrying the ball was a spin move, which I did, but as I came out of my spin the Hesperia cornerback came flying over the top and lit my fire. I saw a flash then darkness for a split second. I blacked out, came too, and got back in the huddle. I wasn't the same after that. I remember my father having to wake me up every hour or so that night to make sure I wasn't in a coma.

Nonetheless, the season continued. We ended our 1995 season with a hard fought, but worthless 3-

7 record. No playoff appearance, no championship ring. Although we did have a couple All Citrus Belt League 1st team selections, as well as 2nd team selections in which I was included. All the anticipation and hard work we put in seemed like it was for naught. I learned, however, that even though we didn't have a winning season, **hard work and dedication is never for naught**. It made us better men. One player received a full scholarship to Utah State; a close teammate of mine that was heavily recruited ended up going to play at Chaffey College in Rancho Cucamonga where he did well and was an all-conference selection two years in a row. We watched the class of 1996 graduate and become adults. As we said goodbye to the Senior class, and got prepared for the next season, we had better things in mind for our class, the Class of 1997!

Priorities

Man cannot live on football alone. In the mid 1990s, just like every other decade, high school was a playground for developed young girls and young men with high testosterone levels. High school, back then, was all about hooking up and trying to score. That's all we talked about as young men and it seemed to be our daily, weekly, and monthly goal. Some sacrificed their studies or football to have more action with the girls.

My reality, on the other hand, was school first, then football, then girls. Since I had a goal to play on Saturday mornings at a Division I school, I had to keep my grades up. So I never put anything before my grades and football. Football and grades were going to be my ticket out of the Inland Empire, out of Victorville especially. This didn't mean, however, that girls were completely off my radar. Junior year, if you remember was the year I lost my virginity. When I wasn't practicing or doing the assigned homework, I was still chasing tail just like everyone else. Working out and building muscle made me popular among the girls, and I discovered that the girls liked my brown eyes and thought I was handsome.

Back then, we didn't have text messages and social media, so we had to talk to each other or make use of pencil and paper. Passing notes was essentially the biggest thing on every campus. You would have your pen pals that you wrote letters to every period. When the dismissal bell rang, you would exchange letters and read them the next period. I remember the anticipation of receiving a letter from a girl that you liked, hoping she liked you as well. We used to be so excited to get out of class, waiting to receive letters from girls. And then there were the phone calls. Everyone had a home phone or landline. The whole family used that same phone unless their parents decided to get a separate landline for their kids, which some families with a little more income chose to do. Everyone else had to use the family phone. This was when dads would interrogate the boys calling for their daughters. Plenty of times I remember having to explain who I was, and why I was calling to a girl's father or mother. This actually happened when my voice got deep, and some parents were concerned that a grown man was calling their little girl.

Senior Season 1996

After the disappointment of the 1995 season, all the seniors along with the coaches decided that things would have to be different for the 1996 season. We knew that the senior leadership would have to be very intense. We set our hopes high and laid down some attainable team goals as well as individual goals. Our team goals were to beat Eisenhower and Rancho Cucamonga, among the other teams in the preseason, beat all our desert rivals, bring back "The Axe" and "The Bell," win league, go to the playoffs and win a CIF championship. My personal goals for the season were to go all league first team, make the Daily Press All High Desert Team, get All CIF honors, and get that scholarship that I wanted my whole life to a Division I university. Both the team goals and my personal goals were highly attainable, although they would take a tremendous amount of work, will, discipline, and dedication. Our coach was a Notre Dame fan, and an avid fan of Vince Lombardi, whom I believe he adopted most of his coaching philosophy from. As seniors, we took on this philosophy of having the "will to win" and being "mentally tough." We were ready to put it down.

We knew that we had to push the envelope a little more than everyone else for two reasons. Reason number one was that we all wanted to play on Saturday mornings on a college team in front of massive crowds. Number two was that we wanted to graduate successful, winning all our desert rival games and then some. At Victor Valley High School, among alumni, if you can say you graduated with "The Bell" and "The Axe," that set you apart from ordinary alumni that can't say the same. For the past few years we never had the coveted axe and the bell was taken from us in '94 due to technicalities and we lost the game in '95. We were on a clear mission to put the class of '97 on the forefront of all the other graduating classes. We wanted to be legends in the hallways.

Spring football came in May, which was a blast because we were all so excited about the upcoming 1996 football season. Scouts had been coming to our school, talking to us individually, and sending letters. I had been receiving recruitment letters since my sophomore year. By now I had a couple shoe boxes full of letters from different schools including Nebraska, Colorado, Northwestern, all the service academies, and several other Division I, II and III schools. I knew this was just a formality and that it wasn't time to get happy, although it was a confidence booster. Some days we would come to spring practice and there would be scouts there or newspaper press. We had a fist full of prospects on our team. Including myself, our six foot, four inch wide receiver/free safety, our corner, linebacker and a couple underclassmen that were getting lots of looks from scouts.

When Hell week came again in 1996, my coach increased it to two weeks, three times per day. He wanted to push us like we had never been pushed before. It was our way of life back then, and we wanted it more than it hurt. We wanted it more than it was uncomfortable; we wanted it more than it was hot. The mental toughness that ran through our green and white blood was at a high level. As a team, we defeated those three-a-day practices and proceeded into the first week of school, which gave us our first game of the season under the lights.

Week 1 - we had Rancho Cucamonga and their zone offensive attack. This attack was led by the leading rusher in the state of California. The past season he had over 24 touchdowns and was an all CIF Southern Section selection. This guy could run, catch, was special on special teams and to top it all off he was incredible at cornerback. The previous year he had given our team a work over and we were determined not to let that happen again. What makes this game stand out in my head after all these years is that right before we took the field we heard that the young talented rapper that wrote "All Eyes on Me" who was fatally shot the previous week, had just died. To our generation at the time, it was like the President dying. Still, we had to keep going, and be prepared to take the field and give Rancho Cucamonga a long painful death of their own. At halftime the scoreboard read 13-13. It was Friday, the 13th, an unusually unlucky day historically, and the score was tied at 13. Nevertheless, as hard as we fought that night, we couldn't overcome that Rancho Cucamonga team.

Week 2 - we got totally smashed by Bloomington High School, who in the mid 90s rolled up most teams with a powerful double wing offense. This squad had numerous threats, led by a head coach that was not afraid to put 100 points on the opposing team if they couldn't stop their double wing attack. We prepared for this game all week, emulating the double wing offense with the scout team, but to no avail. Despite an awesome effort, I ran a kickoff back 94 yards and had a reception for a touchdown, they beat us with a score of 70-20.

Week 3 - we won a game over Highland High School of Palmdale, which made our record 1-2. We proceeded into week 4 against Eisenhower High School of Rialto, California. As I have mentioned previously, I always loved to play Eisenhower because it was located in my hometown in which I grew up and went to elementary and junior high school. A lot of my buddies from junior high school played on the Eisenhower team. However, in 1994 and 1995, Eisenhower smashed us by at least 20-30 points. The 1996 season would be the year that we ran with them and came out victorious.

Week 4 was game day against Ike. *The Star Spangled Banner* played, the ball was kicked and the war started. It was intense, and every play was a struggle for a few yards. You could tell that they were struggling to maintain their running game in spite of their number one guy's absence. Likewise, we were trying to match our total offensive attack despite the absence of our 6 foot 4 inch quarterback who didn't make the trip. It was a beast in the trenches. Ike's speedy and tenacious 4-4 defense would not let us get outside on our sweeps, and their hungry linebackers were shutting down the middle. At one point during the game, my coach accused me of not playing hard. I said he was crazy because I had dreamed of this game for a whole year. I was playing hard, but they were also playing hard. Two teams battling it out; no room for mistakes. Every time my tight end blocked down, I would fill and smash the running back. They persisted; then finally they ran a counter play and scored from 30 yards out. It was 7-0 at halftime. We weren't panicking, but we were thirsty for a win over this powerhouse.

Halftime was over and the battle proceeded.

Big hits, hard fought yards, and a constant struggle for pride and respect on both sides of the ball. We could not get into the end zone against the stingy, and very fast Eisenhower defense. We played tight defense ourselves. Finally, late in the game, they chose to run an out and up against our star corner. Needless to say, he bit on the out and the receiver went deep. The crowd stood up, the ball was in the air as the receiver caught it and ran towards the end zone, but then he began to high step from the 20-yard line. He embarrassed us. In the mid-1990s the high step was the ultimate disrespect in the game of football. Not only had they chose us for homecoming, now this cat was high stepping into the end zone on us. It wasn't time to worry at this point but we had to put some points on the board as soon as possible. We never gave up, but we never scored in that game. A hard fought battle, and respect earned, but we lost. We were mad about the loss, but happy that it was only by two touchdowns.

Week 5 - we played Moreno Valley High School of Moreno Valley, California. They were always a team full of brothers with good speed and heart. This particular year they ran the Wishbone. The Wishbone was an offense from the 1980s that had been put to rest by most offensive coordinators. The offense had been completely figured out. All week we planned our attack and defense. In the wishbone, there are three threats; the dive, the off tackle play and the quarterback/tailback option. Our plan was to have a linebacker designated to tackle the dive every play no matter if he had the ball or not, have someone hit the quarterback every play, and for me to hit the pitch man every single play of the game. Moreno Valley came in ready, but after four quarters of football, we had dominated them and shut down their outdated wishbone offense. It was a good win for the Victor Valley football team. We needed the uplift going into week 6, which would start league play and most importantly be the 1996 renewal of The Bell Game.

1996 Bell Game

Any decade, any year, month or week, there is one thing for sure about a Victor Valley football team, and that is there is no problem getting hyped up for the Bell game. This game, no matter what, is the single most important event in the High Desert, outside of probably the high school graduation. And it would still be a close second to the graduation only because education comes first. The type of hype that was centered around the game made the players feel like superstars or celebrities. We knew for a fact that at least 5,000 people would be in those stands watching us battle it out for the bell.

The Monday before the game my coach reminded me of what happened the previous year at the Bell Game when Apple Valley's wide receiver took me deep and embarrassed me by back pedaling into the end zone after I had fell while guarding him. He knew I wanted a do over to prove myself this time around. This was it, my last Bell Game, and I wanted to make the most out of it and bring that precious bell back to its green and white home. The anticipation and excitement swarmed through the school, from the youngest freshmen, to the oldest senior, including the administration and teachers.

Finally, Friday night was here. We were in pre-game awaiting the 7:30pm kickoff. Under the lights at Ray Moore Stadium, you could see our giant letter "V" lit up on the mountain to the east of the school. The Apple Valley side of the stadium was already filled to capacity. The coveted bell was on their sideline spray painted orange and black. "Ding dong, ding dong," the bell rang out loud. That intense ring created an almost conditioned response of excitement, anticipation, and goose bumps. We looked at the opposition; they returned the gaze with intensity.

As the *Star Spangle Banner* played, and the cymbals rang out to the beat of the song, we stood resolute, with our helmets in our hands ready for the upcoming dogfight. And a dogfight it was. My assignment was to shut down their star player. They wasted no time testing me. Their first offensive snap they tried to pick on me. He lined up wide to the left, I got in a low but agile defensive back stance slightly inside of him to take away the inside route. The ball was snapped, he faked outside, I honored it just a little bit and then he switched directions and broke for the inside on a slant. I quickly recovered and ran with him full speed. When he looked up, I looked up and the quarterback was releasing the ball. Time slowed down as the ball approached his hands. I was trailing him, staying on top of the route as the ball hit his hands. I batted the ball down with my left hand as I took him to the ground with my right hand. It fell incomplete. With confidence, I jumped up with enthusiasm. "Not today," is what I yelled out with passion. Throughout the entire first half of the game they kept going back to him, but to no avail. I was all over him like white on rice, only thinking of the previous year when he embarrassed me in the 32-21 loss inside T. Bass Stadium.

At halftime we had a 13-10 lead over Apple Valley, but we knew that a rivalry this huge, this anticipated, almost never came without a serious drawn out fight. We still had another half of football to play in which anything could happen. We rallied our troops, got an earful from the coaches about the mistakes we may have done, and got ready to get back on the gridiron to seal that envelope once and for all. At the second half of the game both teams fought and persisted for the entire third quarter of the game. The score was still 13-10, in spite of all the big runs and great plays that were happening. No one was getting into the end zone. All we had to do was keep Apple Valley out of the end zone and we would go away with the bell and a sweet victory to start us off right in Mojave River League play. But we already knew that it wouldn't be that simple. With a little under two minutes left in the fourth quarter of the game, Apple Valley began to rally and get some swag. Their sidelines and crowd were ranting and yelling, and routing them on. The bell was ringing out loudly as if a train was getting ready to pull into a station. It created a thirst and a hunger in us; it was our motivation.

Back on offense, their wide receiver lined up wide right as the crowd cheered on the rally. The quarterback called the snap and he took off with a purpose up the sideline. I just knew he was going to go deep. I was right with him on his hip, running, waiting for the ball to go up, but in a split second I realized that he was only trying to run me off for a run play. As I heard my defense yell, "Run!" I stopped to come back to the play. The play was off tackle to my side. I came up hard only to meet his opposition. I was strong and shifty and gave him a move plus threw him off of me. The running back was on his way up the sideline and I was the last man between him and the end zone. He ran, then, I ran to him with a clear shot to knock his block off. The contact was made; he got low and ran right through me. I missed the tackle. He sprinted like a world-class sprinter to the end zone. The Victor Valley crowd sat down; the Apple Valley crowd jumped and hugged each other.

As their team celebrated, only negative thoughts entered my head. I messed up again, and let Apple Valley come back. Forever I would be remembered for this loss. I snapped back into it and got ready for the two-point conversion. They missed the two-point conversion and it was time for kick off with just about a minute to play. There was still hope.

I would be lying if I told you that I didn't have any doubts. I had some doubts, but the time didn't allow me to dwell on the negatives. Our coach showed his leadership by not concentrating on the mistake that I had just made, but instead rallying us and motivating us to use this minute that remained the best possible way we could. After the kick off we came out throwing. The first play after the kick we went deep to our go-to guy, but our z-back caught it in his stead. We jumped for joy with happiness. This moved the ball to about the 40-yard line. We came back with another pass play, complete just below the 20-yard line. We ran two different plays that pushed us right up to the ten-yard line, but we couldn't get into the end zone. Then, our coach called a time out.

Here we were, with seconds left on the clock, looking into the end zone from about the ten-yard line, with a chance to score and pull off one of the biggest come back victories in Bell Game history. When we huddled on the sidelines during the timeout I remember looking into my coach's eyes as he spoke and let us know the plan. He told us to stay poised and that we weren't going to let these Apple Valley "bastards" come over here and "whoop are ass in our own house." I remember him saying, "We are Victor Valley, the only reason we flush our toilets is so Apple Valley can have drinking water." He was angry. His plan was that when we went up to the line of scrimmage check and saw their defense position, then we would do one of two things: If they came out in a 4-4 defense, run 8 sweep; if they come out in a 5-2 defense, run the quick slant to our go-to guy. The plan was solid. It was either going to myself, or the quick slant to our go-to guy, who was about 6 foot 4 inches. The referee blew the whistle and time out was over. We trotted to the line of scrimmage with the plan clearly in our heads. I was excited, nervous, and determined. If they came out in a 4-4 I would have the chance to make up for missing that last tackle.

When Apple Valley's defense lined up, they were in a 5-2 defense. The call was going to our go-to guy. The quarterback started the cadence and time seemed to be ticking extra slowly. He dropped back looking to his right; I stepped up to block on his blind side, and as he released the ball I peeked to see the end result of the game. Our guy stepped quickly to his left, slanted towards the end zone, and the ball was released. There was one Apple Valley defender there, then our guy caught the football as he slid across the end zone on his side. The crowd went wild. There were no flags, and he caught the pass. We were up with only a few seconds remaining. The Victor Valley sidelines erupted with cheers and screaming.

The players started mimicking the sound of the bell: "Ding dong, ding dong" it was coming home. On the field we jumped around with excitement while the Apple Valley defense walked off with disgust. We won the Bell Game that year, my final Bell Game. The score was 19-16 over Apple Valley High School at Ray Moore Stadium. When you win the bell there is a euphoric feeling that enters your body and that feeling lasts for a whole year, sometimes even a lifetime.

Chapter 4

Playoff Bound

After the Bell Game victory, we road that momentum all the way through league play. We persisted and fought the good fight, and we were able to achieve something great. However, we weren't done yet. We swept through the newly formed Mojave River League with ambition and a chip on our shoulder beating Sultana High School in week seven 39-6, Hesperia High School in week eight 21-14, Burroughs High School of Ridgecrest in week nine 26-7, where I had two touchdowns and an interception in that game. We even brought home "The Axe" from Barstow High School, beating them 41-6 on a very cold, bloody and windy November night in Barstow.

A season that started off very rough ended up coming together after a lot of hard work, discipline, determination, and 6 a.m. practices in the ice-cold Victor Valley mornings before school. We had finally become 7-3, Mojave River League champions, and on our way to the playoffs. Our school hadn't been to the playoffs in ten years. We would be playing La Quinta High School, a number three seed, in the first round.

In the first round of the playoffs we rolled up La Quinta High School with a score of 59-0. Some of the coaches from my sophomore year were now coaching at La Quinta, which turned out to be quite a headline for the media. That was one down and three to go. Next up was Norte Vista High School of Riverside, California. Norte Vista was the first seed in their league and was known for their big 6 foot 5 inch receiver who had been giving all the other teams a run for their money all season. Thankfully, we planned for this and destroyed Norte Vista by a score of 31-0. The school couldn't believe it; the community couldn't believe it. The newspapers reported, with surprise, that Victor Valley would be on its way to the semi-final game of the Division 8 playoffs. If we won the upcoming game against Pacific High School of San Bernardino, California we would be in the championship game. All we could think about was getting championship rings.

Saturday in films we watched Pacific High School, the team we were set to play next. They had three running backs, all over 200 pounds, and they could all run like they weighed 170. They had a free safety, the son of a local USC standout and 49er, who was big and could run and hit. (His dad actually played with my uncle at USC in the late 1970s and early 80s, and they were both on that 1978 National Championship team.) In addition to the three running backs and the quarterback, they had a fast all-league receiver. The bottom line was that they were stacked, but we were also stacked and felt as if we could take them down. We had speed, size, and strength as well, and still had a chip on our shoulders.

We wanted to get past Pacific and possibly get a rematch against the same Bloomington team in the championship that beat us by 50 points in week two. Coaches devised a plan and we went to work on Monday, running a lot of sweeps. On the second day of practice, while I was running an eight sweep, my hamstring popped. Even the coaches heard it from the sidelines. I wouldn't let this derail me from playing on Saturday night. Coaches just decided they would save me for defense, since I had a bad wheel. I was very upset about my hamstring, but was determined to give my all in an effort to win this ring we all so fondly dreamed of.

Saturday night came quickly. The newspapers had been hyping the game up all week, favoring Pacific High School because of their three-man attack at running back, superstar receiver, and quarterback. Not to mention, the schools down the hill were always expected to beat the schools from the High Desert. Unfortunately, this usually turned out to be correct. But we were the dream team, V-Hi's finest. It was going to be different this time.

It was a short bus ride down the hill that felt drawn out simply because of the anxiety levels that are tied into the C.I.F. Playoffs and playing for a possible chance to go to the championship game and put it all on the line for one of those fabulous rings that everyone talks about. I wanted mine to be yellow gold with diamonds. Much of the anticipation also came from knowing that my whole family would be in the stands— Mom, Dad, brothers, and a host of other relatives, including my grandmother, who were always proud of me.

When we arrived at Pacific High School, the security opened the gates and the famous "P" on the side of the mountain that I looked at my whole life growing up was lit up and meant something totally different to me this time. As a kid I used to marvel at the sight of that "P" on the mountain, but tonight that letter stood for something totally different and was not marvelous anymore. It was the stamp of the enemy; the team that was trying to stop us in our tracks from accomplishing our goal of winning a championship. We were dressed in our all white jerseys with green numbers, and white pants with a thick green stripe on the side, similar to Michigan State's uniforms in the early to mid 90s. Green helmets with the white stripe down the middle and all of my stickers started at the front of my helmet and went back like I had seen all the college players do. My jersey was precisely tucked and taped so that my six-pack abs would be visible if I went up for an interception. There was silence in the locker room for the traditional five-minute meditation, in which everyone closed their eyes and thought about their assignments. This was a mental practice we performed before every game where each player would go through every offensive and defensive play or assignment in their heads.

After early outs, the linemen and non-specialty guys would come out the locker room for stretching and the normal pre-game activities. I remember looking at the coaches, thinking this one is ours. Our coaches walked around with confidence and assurance. Ten minutes before kickoff we would take that long walk back to the locker room for final speeches, prayers and hype. **"Think that you can and you will."** is what my head coach always preached.

I went out with my co-captains for the coin flip and they won the toss but elected to kick to us and defer until the second half of the football game. They lined up in all Purple, kicking away from their scoreboard towards Perris Hill Park to the north of their campus. We returned to the south, looking at the scoreboard. The kick was off and it soared high and deep right to me. I caught it, took three steps up, and turned to my right for the reverse. As I approached the other deep back for the reverse, I got a feeling and I cut up field avoiding the reverse and the picket that was set up for me on their sideline. It felt like Moses had parted the Red Sea. I turned it on, listening to the crowd cheer and my sideline yell, "Go!" Seventy-eight yards later I was pulled down from behind by one of their speedsters. I was surprised I got that far with my bum hamstring, but I was fired up. Three plays later we were in the end zone. Touchdown! We were up 7-0 after the PAT.

The Pacific team were no slouches either. On their ensuing possession, they marched down the field in their power offense and capped the drive off with a thirty yard run right up the middle. We were in a cover two, I was on one hash and my free safety was on the other. When the ball was snapped, all we saw was a big flash right between us. This was not going to be an easy road. Pacific was fast and tough. Their record was 10-1-1 coming into this match, and ours was 9-3 respectively. It was definitely going to be a dogfight. The game was now 7-7. The whole first half our teams went back and forth. It was an intense, hard hitting half. And when the gun sounded to end the first half, the score was 17-17.

The momentum seemed to be split even and we were feeling good as a team. I remember walking back to the locker room at halftime thinking to myself, "We got this next half, it's on!" At halftime, our coaches did their usual thing, going over adjustments, praising those that were worthy and cussing out and yelling at those who weren't. Nevertheless, instead of dwelling on the past, we needed to focus on the second half of the game.

The second half started and ended before we

could blink. The Pacific High School Pirates intensified their game in the second half and rolled up 24 unanswered points. With about two minutes left on the clock I started to realize that this was it. This was the end of a short but glorious season, and high school career. Coach put me in for the last couple offensive possessions, blown hamstring and all, because we needed a prayer. In a desperate attempt to score one for the Gipper, coach called our last and final play, "9 Sweep Pass." Set, go. I took the handoff, faking sweep towards our sideline, pulled up and threw the deep ball as far as I could throw it as I got hit from different directions. The ball went up in a spiral, but the Pacific defense came down with it. Interception. Signed, sealed, and delivered. The game was over.

The Pacific Pirates had defeated the Victor Valley Jackrabbits 41-17 in the Division VIII semi finals. I was heartbroken, and couldn't hide my emotions. We cried as a team, we fought together as a team; we persevered through every play as a team. We scored and were scored upon. When the final gun sounded, we were in the middle of the field, some on our knees, some standing up crying together. The feeling of defeat is ice cold. I remember being so sad and angry that I raised my middle finger with contempt. I didn't know what else to do. By this time our friends and families had come down to the field to console us. As we grieved painfully, there was a celebration going up on the other side of the field. It was a scene where we were both celebrating life and death at the same time. **In life you win some and you lose some. Well we had lost, there was no tomorrow. This was the end.**

Signing Day

Once football season ended, recruiting season began. College scouts traveled from all over the country or their designated recruiting areas to seek out the best athletes that were academically and athletically eligible. My hard work and determination had paid off in the form of a 1st Team All Mojave River League selection, The Daily Press Football Defensive Player of the Year Award, The 1996 Victor Valley Football Most Valuable Player Award, The 1996 Topper Patterson Memorial Award recipient, The 1996 "Bell Game" Defensive Player of the Game Award and a host of other acknowledgements that were presented to me as well. Although I had not received an All C.I.F Southern Section selection or a San Bernardino Sun All Area selection, I thought my chances were looking splendid for obtaining a football scholarship.

It had been my dream to be able to play college football for a university. I would give anything to be able to suit up and play a game on a Saturday morning in front of thousands of fans, in a major stadium like the Rose Bowl, the Coliseum, Superdome or Jack Murphy Stadium. My first recruiting letter came when I was a sophomore in high school from the University of Colorado. I was honored. As time progressed, I received letters from over 50 different colleges and universities across the country. Some of these letters were from schools like Nebraska, Oklahoma State, Northwestern, UCLA, and all of the Military Academies. Now that I was a senior in high school, the recruiting process started to narrow down. It was not about getting to know you anymore; the recruiting process was now all about who they really wanted. Schools started dropping off the face of the earth at this point. In December of 1996 and January of 1997 there were only a few schools left that were actually considering offering me a scholarship. The University of Idaho, Stanford, Northwestern University and Oklahoma State were the only schools still calling my house and coming to my school to pull transcripts and talk with me and my coaches. With an SAT score of 1100 out of 1600 and a 3.1 GPA, I was ready to go and had already been cleared by the National Clearinghouse.

I was astounded when Stanford University's recruiter told me he would be mailing me a paper application to fill out as soon as possible in order to keep the process going. The recruiter from the University of Idaho made frequent trips to my school to speak with me. Of course it made me feel special that these schools really wanted me. I could only imagine playing in front of 100,000 fans at a major stadium representing my last name, and my city. It was a glorious thought. I was blessed just to have made it this far. Most student-athletes never get phone calls from colleges and never even get recruited. In fact, most athletes are done for good after high school. Playing in college was my dream and I was getting closer and closer to realizing that dream.

To my dismay, the closer we got to the February 7th signing date, the less calls I received from scouts. I had begun to worry. Some of the scouts disappeared and never contacted me again. Some other scouts were more courteous about the situation. I remember receiving a phone call from Stanford saying that they wouldn't be recruiting me anymore because I had too many C's on my transcripts. The Idaho recruiter told me that he was looking at another guy in Moreno Valley, California, and he was their first choice. If in fact this guy turned down their offer, they would offer me the scholarship as a second choice. It didn't feel good being second in line, but it was a little appealing. In the end, the guy in Moreno Valley took the scholarship. Then, I was left with no one calling my house, no trips scheduled, and considering going to a junior college. The only great thing about the junior college option was that I would be able to sign with a Division I school right after my freshman season. I was still left feeling depressed even though I had some reasonable options. The depression came from having hopes high, working my hardest, having faith, then getting let down and abandoned by all the hopefuls in the end. It was a terrible feeling being on campus as the star football player and not having an answer when someone asked, "So where are you going to be playing next year?" And believe me, every day of the week, no matter where I was, someone asked me that question. I had no answer for them.

The ASB bookkeeper and our Vice Principal at the time, an African American man, even tried to help me out by taking me to the Soul Awards in Los Angeles. These awards had been set up to honor football players from historically black colleges and universities. They thought it may be a great way to network with some of the coaches that would be in attendance. They went as far as setting up the tickets, renting me a tux and driving me down there to attend the ceremony. I attended and met plenty of football legends in attendance, such as one of the only Black men to quarterback for the University of Southern California and lead them to Rose Bowl wins, later went on to the pros, and the 6 foot 4 inch running back from the Cleveland Browns that wrecked havoc in the 50s and 60s that later went on to become an actor. As an 18-year-old young Black man, this served as one of the highlights of my life.

I kept working out and lifting weights, believing that I would get picked up late in the game. February's signing date, by this point, had come and went. Everyone that had accepted scholarships had already signed to their respective schools and their write up in the paper had already been released. I always dreamed of signing a national letter of intent to accept a scholarship, and getting featured in the local paper.

Months went by and it seemed that my only options were to choose from smaller schools like Mt. San Antonio College, Chaffey College, or walking on at Cal Berkeley or UC Davis that I had been accepted to already academically. I was leaning towards going to Cal Berkeley because most of my family were encouraging me to go there. I didn't know at the time that Cal was the number one public college in the country. All I knew was that they had a football team, and they were in the Pac 10, and that was all that seemed to matter.

Late in March, after track practice, I was walking through the football office and my head coach asked me a question that changed my life. He asked, "Have you ever considered playing football for one of the academies?" I said, "No." The ironic thing about this question was that ever since I was a sophomore I had been throwing away the letters and questionnaires from all the academies. I grew up Jehovah Witness, and my mother always told me it was wrong to go to the military, only she never told me exactly why. Nonetheless, I never paid attention to the letters and communications that I received from military academies like the Army, Naval, and Air Force Academy. I told my coach that I had never even considered it an option. It turns out that the Army Academy at West Point saw a film of me and was interested. They were coming to Victorville to see me. I was shocked, but I wasn't interested.

Army Comes Knocking!

Within the next day or so the Army Football recruiter called my house to introduce himself and get a feel for me. I talked with him and told him that I had never considered going to the Army, let alone one of the military academies. He told me he wanted to see if I would give him a chance to state his case for the Army and see if it just might be a fit. They had already pulled all my transcripts and talked with all my coaches. He set up a time with my dad and stepmom to come to my house and put everything on the table. In the back of my head I'm thinking, "Wow, if he's coming to the house, they mean business." No recruiter comes to sit down knee-to-knee with you and your parents if they're not serious.

I was more flattered than I was appreciative that the Army really wanted me. So the next week the recruiter showed up at my house all the way from New York State to Victorville, California to try and sell me on their academy. When he sat down at the table he did most of the talking, and selling. The one

105

thing that I heard and I'll never forget he said was when he started talking about ring knockers. Everyone that graduates from West Point gets a fancy, blinged out ring and when they slap their hands on the table, the ring makes this loud noise. It was a sacred tradition. It may seem trivial, but I placed a lot of value on going to college and getting a ring.

He began telling me all the things I didn't want to hear about academy life, the five-year commitment, the lack of social life, and the basic training. All I focused on was when he said, "The 1996 Army Football team beat Notre Dame and went on to win a bowl game." This was the last rabbit he pulled out his hat as a selling point. The Army Football team beat Notre Dame and won a bowl game just last season. And they wanted me to come out there and play for them! I started to get excited although not thoroughly convinced. He showed me the bowl ring and the media guide from the bowl game. I was impressed. Then he dropped the bomb on me telling me that they wanted to fly me out to New York to visit West Point next week, which would be the weekend of April 4th. Through all my recruiting calls, letters, and lead-on's, I had never been offered a trip by any school. In recruiting, if a school offers you a trip, they are ready to sign you. So this is when it all started sinking in. I started imagining myself playing in the historic Army vs. Navy game, and being in the Army, and all kinds of other thoughts started flooding my brain. There was finally a light at the end of the recruitment tunnel.

My dad was ecstatic. He was a man that wanted to join the Marines when he was eighteen years old, but they wouldn't let him because of his scoliosis. He always wanted to be a military man and thought this was the opportunity of a lifetime for me. I really didn't understand back then how prestigious West Point was. But I still had my reservations. A military academy would be very different from any other university. Everyone at the school, including my coach, was telling me how great of an opportunity it was and what my life would be like if I attended the academy. Finally my head coach organized a sit down with one of the other coaches who just so happened to be an enlisted Army recruiter. He set up a time where we would go out to lunch and discuss it.

He took me out to pizza and we talked for about an hour or so about why I should go to West Point. As I stuffed my face with pizza, I listened carefully to what he had to say. He convinced me to at least go on the trip with an open mind. I obliged. So we set the trip up for April 4th-6th. I flew into Newark, New Jersey where a coach from Army picked me up and drove me upstate about an hour to West Point. I flew out of Ontario International Airport to Newark. When we arrived at West Point, I remember how scenic and beautiful it was. It was like a fort being built right in the middle of the woods. It's right off the west point of the Hudson river. The Hudson river was massive, flowing with greatness. We drove around the huge campus and passed Michie Stadium. The hair on my arms rose up as we passed the historic stadium, full of tradition. I showered, cleaned up and had a fancy steak and shrimp meal at the West Point Hotel before going to the football offices to meet the head coach of the program and take a tour of the football offices.

The head coach, and some of the other coaches, were surprised of my size. I guess they thought I looked smaller on film. I met up with some other recruits and got a tour of the facility. I still wasn't sure at that point, but by the end of the trip, and all the food and accommodations, I had pretty much made my mind up that I was going to go.

I asked one of the coaches if there were any fraternities on campus. My brother was a part of Omega Psi Phi Fraternity, Incorporated and I had decided that I wanted to be a part of that organization as well when I got to college. When the coach told me that some of the guys on the football team had joined some frat, but he didn't know which one it was, I crossed my fingers. Later that day, when we met some of the team, I asked around and happily found out that the same frat my brother was in, these guys on the football team were also in. I was sold. I made up my mind at that point that I was going to West Point to be a part of the long gray line and play

Army football.

When I made it back to Victorville I started the application process for West Point and all the extra requirements needed to be a part of this glorious institution. I had to also get a nomination from a California Congressman and take all types of physicals test. We were working with limited time since they started recruiting me so late in the game. The recruiter told me that if things didn't work out I'd be a shoe in for the United States Military Academy Prep School, and could enter West Point the next year. Even so, everything was finalized for me to attend West Point.

It's Official

When it became official that I was going to West Point it was like someone set off fireworks in the High Desert. It was this super big deal. I was still oblivious to the fact that West Point was compared to an Ivy League institution and was possibly harder to get into than a Harvard, Yale or Stanford. Everyone was telling me these things, but the academic excellence and credibility of West Point didn't register to me at first because I took it for granted. In the back of my head I appreciated the fact that someone wanted me for my football prowess and was willing to give me a shot. That is what I really appreciated.

In early May my coach told me that the Daily Press wanted to do an article on me about my accepting a scholarship to play football at West Point. This was what I was waiting for my whole life – to have my name on the front page of the sports section telling the world that I had signed with a major Division I college. It may be vanity, or ego that drove me this far, but there was almost nothing as exciting as getting your name and picture on the front page of the Sports section.

On May 8th, 1997 the biggest article of my life hit the press and let the world know I had made it. "Henderson Headed to West Point: Victor Valley Defensive Back Becomes a Cadet" is what the title read. Throughout my career at Victor Valley High School I saw only a handful of football players receive this honor. This really made me feel wanted and accepted among the football world, especially after the light depression I experienced after not being recruited by lots of schools. I read this article over and over again. I smiled and reminisced about how I used to be a young boy at my Granny's house looking at all my uncle's trophies and accolades. I thought about his Fiesta Bowl Plaque, and his Tommy the Trojan Senior Award from USC. I thought about all the days that I ran around with my football as a young boy looking for someone to play catch with. All the love and passion that I was able to maintain for football over the years was, at that point, about to pay off in a major way. My dream was finally being realized.

When the article hit the stands everyone in the community, especially at the high school, had nothing but positive things to say about me and well wishes. I remember walking through the school halls and teachers that I never had the privilege of having a class with even knew who I was and acknowledged my accomplishment. The ASB bookkeeper (who helped me out tremendously) and our one African American male administrator (Oregon State Alum) who had served as a mentor to me and other black males on campus were also very proud of me. It was like overnight with the acceptance of the Military Academy, I had become the pride of Victorville and Victor Valley High School.

Many people throughout the community would ask me if I was the same guy that was in the paper getting ready to attend West Point. I would smile and nod yes. They would tell me how hard it is to get in there and stay there, I agreed. But once I started something I had to finish it. I always thanked people for their well wishes. It made me feel very proud that my city had my back and I would be representing Victorville, the Inland Empire, and California way out on the East Coast. My father always said that everything worth doing is hard. This would be hard, but I was ready.

Class of 1997

Graduation came quickly. However, right before graduation was an event that was equally just as important to me— the Mr. Jackrabbit Contest. This was an underwear contest, talent contest, and a group dance contest for the male seniors. Each contestant would be judged accordingly by a panel of judges and all the girls in the school would be in the front row lusting. I had watched previous Mr. Jackrabbit contest in the past and knew that my senior year I wanted to be named Mr. Jackrabbit. Needless to say, I spent all of my senior year preparing for that contest – working out at the gym for two hours afterschool with a bodybuilder. The only thing I had left to prepare was my talent. I decided I would sing.

The group dance and the underwear competition turned out great— the girls and some ladies went wild. For my talent I came out in my dad's brim and a black shirt unbuttoned all the way down. My dance was risqué and edgy, but turned out to be a huge success when I claimed the title of Mr. Jackrabbit 1997.

While making preparations for the end of the senior year events like senior pictures and graduation, my dental record results came back from West Point and I found out I had to get my bottom two wisdom teeth pulled in order to be admitted into the academy. I wasn't excited about having to do it, but my love for the game of football was extreme and I knew I had to do it just so I could play college football. I can still remember the pain of getting my teeth extracted; every part of my face was swollen. Luckily, my senior pictures still came out OK and my jaw had made it back to normal size before graduation.

Graduation day was on June 19, 1997 at Ray Moore Stadium, Victor Valley High School in Victorville, California. Ray Moore Stadium meant so much to me at the time and still does. It was finally my turn to sit there in midfield, in front of all the faculty, family and friends, and get ready to accept my diploma. I was ranked in the top 100 out of 800 graduates so I was sitting near the front of the stage. I was walking with a friend that shared the "Biggest Flirt" title with me in the yearbook. Everyone was proud and ready to journey to the next stage of their lives.

When I crossed the stage I felt liberated. I felt accomplished. But I knew that this was just the beginning. In nine days I would be entering Cadet Basic Training at the United States Military Academy. I was excited and a little intimidated, but confident. After our infamous dog pile at midfield, a fellow classmate sang our class song, "*Keep Your Eyes on the Prize.*" A friend and I have coined this phrase since

1997. The phrase "Keep your eyes on the prize" has continued to be an inspiration for us to this day. We vowed to forever keep our eyes on the prize. Our families and friends came onto the field to congratulate us. My whole family was there. My grandmother was there, being that it was a time before she got sick with dementia, it remains a proud memory.

After enduring some unfortunate times as a child, growing up in a single parent home and having a low-socioeconomic status, I was able to stay focused on a dream and a passion that brewed within me since day one. This dream to play football motivated me to set large goals, and smaller attainable goals, and to see it through to the end. Even as I had to leave my mother's nest, and leap out on faith to a more independent lifestyle at my father's house in a city that I didn't know very well, the dream stayed alive. **The dream kept me laser focused on the bigger picture, keeping the end in sight.** This laser focus guided me on the path less traveled and in the right direction of prioritizing school, athletics and healthy decisions, instead of the more frequented path that consist of piss poor efforts, excuses, and poor decisions.

My graduation was very much a sign of focus and perseverance. It stood as a reminder to others that would come after me, that no matter what your circumstances, if you believe in your dream and are duly passionate, it will lead you to success. This milestone was a major success on the path to my ultimate goal of playing major Division I college football and receiving a college degree. High school graduation was closure to adolescence and the beginning of manhood. Furthermore, it reminded me that proper pre-planning and a great work ethic will always pay off if you keep your eyes on the prize. I did it! No one could ever strip me of this accomplishment; I would be forever initiated into the class of 1997!

CHAPTER 5

West Point

After graduation some of my good friends and I decided to get tattoos. I got a wolf on my chest symbolizing being "Head of the pack." I was scheduled to fly out of Ontario International Airport to Newark, New Jersey on June 28, 1997— exactly nine days after my graduation. Before leaving my plan was to have as much fun as possible. The plan was to throw the biggest house party in the world as a going away party. A friend's mom agreed to let us use her house for the party as long as we made sure the party goers didn't tear her house up. We obliged. We made fliers and passed them out to people from Victor Valley High, Apple Valley High and Hesperia High. The party was going up! We had a DJ with lots of food and lots of people.

After the party, and a few days left before it was time for me to leave, I had to buy some low quarter military shoes, set up a bank account at Bank of America for my direct deposits once I got to Army, and a few other things. My friend and his mother took me to a military surplus store where I got my low quarter shoes and some aviator sunglasses. Then, my stepmother took me to the bank to set up my checking account. I was now ready to go, and the anticipation was killing me. I was ready to go in with all my heart and passion, represent my last name well, and make my family proud.

Finally, June 28th came and I was ready to leave. Before leaving, I spent time with my entire family who gave me words of advice and love. Then I headed to the Ontario International Airport where I would be taking a shuttle flight to LAX and then a red eye flight straight into Newark, New Jersey.

My mother waited with me while I kept watch, hoping that my father would make it to the airport as well. I always had a deep love for my dad, and cherished the many lessons he taught me about manhood and responsibility. This was a huge step in my life and I wanted him to be there with me.

Then they made the last call for passengers to board the plane. I looked around for any signs of my dad, hugged my mother and stalled a little bit. With tears beginning to build up in my eyes, I hugged my mother and boarded the plane with the one little bag that was allowed for me to bring. I sat on the plane with tears in my eyes. I could only think of my father and where he could possibly have been. I looked through the windows of the airport, watching my mom and my little niece, then, suddenly my father appeared running into the waiting area with my stepmother. He was too late, and I could tell he was disappointed.

I always wondered what my father was saying to my mother when he got to the waiting area and saw that I had already boarded. I wondered what he felt in his heart when he didn't get the chance to say good-bye. I never talked about it after that. It was time to get on with my life and my new goals; it was now my job to apply all the lessons of manhood that took place previously.

Beast Barracks

The United States Military Academy had shuttle vans at the airport waiting on all the incoming cadets. These shuttle buses gave all the cadets a ride to a major hotel where we would all be held until the bigger buses from West Point arrived. When I got to the hotel, there were a lot of new cadets already there, talking and joking. I remember being very ready to get this basic training over with so I could start playing football.

The ride to West Point was a quiet and relaxed one until all hell broke loose. "Get up, grab your shit, and get off the bus," an upper-class cadet yelled. This would be the beginning of our eight-week Cadet Basic Training program, affectionately called "Beast Barracks". The term Beast Barracks was very popular because no one ever said Cadet Basic

Training unless it was in a formal setting. As we got off the bus we were immediately ordered to take an enlistment oath that all service members take, swearing to defend the constitution and the country. They told us to grab our bags, follow the yellow lines on the ground, and head straight to the barbershop where everyone would be getting a haircut.

Getting your haircut was not just a beauty statement, it was the Army's way of telling you that you belong to the United States Army now and you'll do what the hell they tell you even if it means sacrificing whatever hair you had. I went in looking different and came out looking like everyone else with my hair completely cut off.

The word "Plebe" rang out from all directions by upper classmen. Plebe is the nickname for new incoming cadets. We wouldn't be recognized as new cadets until we finished basic training, and in April we would be considered real life cadets, if we were lucky. From the barbershop we followed the yellow line to an issuing station where they handed you a huge, and heavy, blue bag and corralled you through this warehouse in which a bunch of civilian workers handed you everything you would ever need in your life. No wonder they only wanted us to bring a change of clothes and some toiletries with us. Most kids leaving for college have a treasure chest, a bunch of blankets and clothes, maybe even a T.V. We, however, all showed up to West Point with a light duffle bag with a change of clothes in it. Everything else we would ever need at the academy would be provided for us, from toothbrushes to combat boots. We also got our battle dress uniforms and our physical training (PT) uniforms, which were the uniforms it seemed we would wear most often. They told us to keep a pair of PT shorts and a PT shirt out with the corresponding socks. Everything they tell you to do is for a reason. Nothing is a surprise to them, although it may be a surprise to you. The next step was ditching our civilian clothes, that we would never see again, and getting changed. We were then placed in our new home or barracks. I was in Washington Barracks, on the fourth floor. These would be temporary barracks until Cadet Basic Training was over. Then, we reported to our upper classmen in charge.

While I was at the academy, the nurses' station is one of the clearest memories I have of new cadet processing because I remember walking in and seeing so many nurses with needles in their hands and a very long line of new cadets. There was an assembly line where they were giving everyone they saw about five shots. I remember getting multiple shots in my right shoulder and multiple shots in my left shoulder. All of it was so new to me. After we got all our shots and clothes it was time for drill.

You don't really appreciate it at the time, because it is so hard on you as a plebe, but the United

States Military Academy is so thorough they teach you how to march and do all the proper military commands in one day. Not saying it is an easy task, but it gets accomplished nevertheless. For hours we drilled, marched, stopped, started, right face, left face, about face and the like. Plebes had to walk noticeably faster than the other cadets –three paces per second is what you would hear the upper class cadets saying. We also had to square every corner. If you were to watch the whole thing in action, it was quite remarkable and a little humorous. Unless of course you were the butt of the joke.

I, along with all other incoming plebes were introduced to the squad leaders who was a cow, or third class cadet that had been through the same process just a year ago. Some of these cows had it in for plebes because they were still holding grudges from the year before. My squad leader was a woman. She was shorter than I, but not evil. As a matter of fact she was a little nurturing. I was in the company Alpha-4, fourth platoon, and fourth squad. We were told to get to know each other really well because we were basically family for the next eight weeks. Everyone received a manual that told us what information we had to learn every day, of every week and prove ourselves proficient in it. The time to prove yourself proficient was when you were in formation awaiting instruction. As the first day of Beast Barracks was ending, we got word through the grapevine that some kids had already quit. I remember thinking to myself that it wasn't even that bad yet. It did serve as a culture shock though, a whole day of people yelling at you and giving you instructions for reasons unknown to you. The unknown is a mind killer. I learned quickly not to worry about the why and just carry out the specific instructions. Lights out was at 2230 hours and you had to be in the bed by 2300 hours because an upper classmen would be on their way to check if you actually broke sheets.

Speaking of sheets, the first day they taught us how to make our beds with hospital corners. The bed had to be so tight and flat you could bounce a quarter off it. I thought the procedure was pretty tight. I never made my bed that tight, but appreciated the new knowledge. Among shining shoes, and keeping your brass spotless throughout the day, keeping your bed tight was something you took pride in. Since you wanted to preserve the tightness of your hospital corners, at night some people would try and sleep on top of their bed so all they had to do in the morning was smooth it over. The upper classmen of course knew this, which is the reason they came in and made sure you broke sheets. The struggle was real.

During the hot and very humid New York summer, we were always stressed to hydrate our bodies so that we would not be a heat casualty the next day. Before we went to bed the first night, our squad leader had us drink 8 canteens of water in preparation for tomorrow's activities in the summer heat. We stood up against the wall with our canteens out just drinking and when you finished one, you held it over your head to get permission to refill it. Then you went to bed. Needless to say I didn't get any sound sleep because I kept having to get up and use the restroom. I often thought this was a secret haze carried down through the years. This was true during the regular evening hours as well. Plebes would stay in their rooms holding their pee and when it got too bad they would gather themselves and embrace the moment of ridicule and critique that you were definitely going to find in the hallways.

The first morning that we had to report to accountability formation was unreal. All anyone ever wanted was sleep, but sleep was not a part of the program. Even when you had free time you weren't supposed to be sleeping. Even at nighttime during lights out there was so much information you had to learn that it didn't make sense to sleep. At 0530 someone came through the halls banging shit and yelling to get up, it was crazy. Accountability formation was at 0545 and breakfast was at 0600. Everyone fell in on the wall outside our room, which was our squad meeting spot. In height order we lined up against the wall and our leader told us what uniform to be in at accountability formation. We had to make sure we got a dress off –it was imperative.

Under all the anxiety and stress that a cadet may take on, forgetting something on your uniform, shining your shoes and brass, and tucking your shirt in properly may go right out the window. The dress off was designed to prevent those mishaps. Cadets that roomed together would make sure to help dress off their roommates and not let them enter the halls of horror looking rather embarrassing. You wanted to make sure your partner first and foremost had on the right uniform. Then you checked to see if the belt buckle was aligned with the zipper and button line on their shirt. You didn't want to have any ranger ropes, which were loose strands of thread that you had to burn off. Shoes shined, brass shined and hat on properly were the most popular reasons to get yelled at.

The squad represented the squad leader so they went through extremes to make sure their squad was thorough. In my 18 years of living, I never practiced getting dressed. At the same time, I never went to West Point. Every day we drilled putting on our uniforms. We would line up on the wall, get instructions, and have 60 - 90 seconds to put on the uniform of our squad leaders choice and line back up on the wall at attention. We got pretty good at this but not without tons of practice. I mean we were getting dressed and undressed for hours at a time it seemed like. I never knew that I could get dressed so fast and meet all the dress off requirements. My favorite uniform of course was the Battle Dress

Uniform or BDU. When I put this uniform on I just felt like a soldier. The aura of confidence and brut strength ran through my blood when I put that uniform on. It was definitely two things going on at this point. We were learning academy and military life and we were transforming our childish ways into characteristics of soldiers.

I was issued so many things in the first week of the academy including a full-fledged computer with internet access. I was happy that I could actually email some of my friends that went on to attend other colleges. I was able to send an email to my next door neighbor to let my dad know I was doing well. When we were issued our M-16A2 assault rifles, I was ecstatic since I always loved guns. When I was reading the pamphlets and watching the videos about West Point as a high school senior, the fact that they had assault rifles was one of the selling points for me. They didn't want to catch you saying gun at the academy. Instead, your assault rifle was your weapon, or you had to call it by its specific name, the Mike 1-6 alpha 2 assault rifle.

Besides learning the basic training of bed making, dressing in my uniform, and assault rifles, what I struggled with the most was the memorization of the entire booklet of military information that included songs, chants, history of the academy, the military rankings for all branches, and much more. Not to mention we always had to know the next three meals on the menu, which meant we had to memorize the daily mess hall menus, plus current events. If an upper classman wanted to know what was going on in the world today we had to be able to tell them. We were being challenged mentally to the fullest extent.

The traditional style of eating for West Point cadets was simply called Cadetiquette. This entailed a wide range of rules used while dining as a Cadet in the mess hall. There was a long list of rules that stuck in my head as peculiar and anal. The Upper-class cadets enjoyed enforcing all the rules they had already internalized. To the uninitiated, it was complete confusion. First of all, when you walk into the mess hall no one can sit down until the whole brigade has entered and is ready to be seated. When you finally sit down, that's when the craziness began. Your knife and fork had to be laid across the top of your plate, and napkins placed in the correct manner. All the food had to be divvied out in equal proportions, and the proper verbal commands used when you wanted something. Everyone had to be sitting there quietly before your table was given permission to eat by the upper-class cadet at your table, and that was just the beginning.

Once you were given the command to start eating, the precise criticism by the head of the table was expected and carried out in full force. You never realize how out of order you are while eating until you go through an etiquette training. We started out eating like primitive cavemen. The upper-classmen would bark orders and stop everyone from eating. The reprimanding was not that bad unless it was directed at you specifically. The fact that no one could eat until everything was done perfectly is what affected everyone else sitting at the table. The first few days I felt like I lost thirty pounds because we never got to eat before time was up. I remember being very frustrated and pondering on sneaking food back in my pocket, which would be considered contraband. If you had food in your barracks, and were found out, you may have to pay the consequences, which stemmed from walking duties to doing laps around my barracks floor, or reciting some information that I was learning at the time.

Physical training was not a problem for me, but I found myself not really putting much effort into learning all the information that I was supposed to. As a matter of fact, most of the kids did more reading and memorization than I had the first day or so. I didn't even know we had to open those books up and start memorizing. My roommates had to clue me in. At the end of the week, we were all supposed to have proved ourselves proficient in the first week's knowledge. When I found this out I got with the program and started getting things checked off while at formation. I believe the first week consisted of simple things like "The Star Spangled Banner." We also had to know how many days until graduation, until Army beat Navy, and until we were recognized as cadets. It was not easy, but it wasn't impossible.

Do not forget that I attended West Point for the sole purpose of playing football. With basic training in full force, football took a quiet back seat. We would resume our football duties when we graduated from basic training. Until then, we only saw the football coaches on Sundays, the day of rest. To my surprise, the head football coach did send out weekly letters of encouragement, which consisted of an Army Football letterhead with and inspirational quote on it signed by himself. I thought I was special in some ways, but I was still humble. Some of the upper class cadets had it out for me knowing I was a football player. I didn't tell them I played football but there aren't too many new cadets that were Black and stood 5'11 inches 191 pounds. I had football written all over my face.

There was a wide range of attitudes in Beast Barracks, but the demographics were pretty set. The majority of the student body was: White Male. Everyone else was a definite minority. There were women in the ranks, but very few; Black women was a scarcity, there were only five that entered Beast Barracks with our class of 2001.

Finally Sunday came, our day of rest. In Beast Barracks, you were given free time on Sundays to worship whatever God you may believe in and get spiritual uplift. They provided various church services for different denominations at the West Point Chapel. If in fact you were like me and didn't want to go to church, you could stay in your room and catch up on knowledge. This wrapped up our first week of being transitioned from civilians to cadets of the United States Army.

Soldiers

I imagine the Cadet Basic Training is different from the enlisted basic training in a few ways, but both have the same intent, which is to make you a responsible, efficient soldier. In Beast Barracks, you not only learn about the Army and how it works but you also learn about the academy and how it specifically works. So in Beast Barracks you're proving yourself worthy to two different entities at the same time, the U.S. Army and the United States Military Academy. Both of these entities are required to produce the same soldiers.

Being trained to be a soldier involves numerous trips to the field in which you learn all types of battle information and receive specific training for various categories. This was mixed into the regimen that we had for academy life. For me, the field was my happy place. Even though we were still going through the same process and living by the same rules, I just felt at home while I was in my battle dress uniform in the field. West Point is a huge place, very beautiful, with vast trees and grassland. We got into formation and marched through fields and forest on our way to different stations. It was all to educate us, even though we didn't process that right away. Walking around with your M16A2 assault rifle like you were in a Vietnam movie was both exciting and real. I enjoyed performing cadences as we marched through holding our weapons.

Over the eight weeks of basic training, we learned how to take apart and put together our weapons in thirty seconds. We learned how to shoot our weapons and had to qualify for marksmanship. As a marksman, you have to qualify standing up, on a knee, in a fox hole, and lying on your stomach. The targets were very far away starting at 100 yards. There were also targets at 200 and 300 yards. When the targets popped up, it was time to shoot. I remember the anticipation of the rifle firing as I tried to gently squeeze the trigger and keep my eyes on center mass. In the military they teach you to shoot center mass. Center mass is from the base of the neck to the waistline. It is actually the biggest target on your body. Everyone is screaming center mass, and making sure your weapons are pointed down range so no one was injured by an accidental gun discharge. It was a great time within a hard time.

We went through obstacle courses, which taught team building, and leadership. I wasn't the tallest in my squad, but by far I was the strongest. So that meant that I was always the first person up the wooden wall. Once I jumped up and sat on the wall, I could pull my whole squad up one by one so we all could make it over the wall. I remember the confidence I felt as I grabbed my squad members and pulled them up. These are quality moments that actually build morale in times of distress. The classic basic training moment was when we had to crawl through mud under barbed wire fence. This taught us how to properly low crawl in the prone position to avoid being killed by rapid fire. The only thing about this is that the mud and water was real. After this drill and obstacle course, everyone was covered with mud and sand, and drenched with water. You could feel mud everywhere, even in your underwear.

Another classic field training station was the gas chamber. This I remembered from watching the West Point video on Cadet Basic Training before I arrived to the academy. All the new cadets were talking about it with anticipation. We previously learned how to seal and lock our gas masks and this field training would be a test of our knowledge and faith in our gas masks. Everyone puts on their gas mask, seals it and locks it in. This is the procedure that allows no air to come in from the sides, only from the filtered front of the mask. You are led into a gas chamber full of tear gas.

When you get in the gas chamber, the military

instructor tells you to notice how you are safe and that nothing is wrong with you. After you realize he's right, he instructs you one at a time to step forward, remove your gas mask, and state your social security number. After seeing the first few cadets choke up and run their ass out of the chamber, except for one dude who was fired up and doing push ups amidst the tear gas, it was my turn. I stepped forward with anxiety, ripped away my gas mask, holding it in one hand and began spitting off my social security number. I was four numbers in when it hit me. Then, it felt like someone punched me in my throat. My eyes, throat and nose were burning with an unknown but terrible sensation. I ran for the door. When I got out the door, that's when the torture started.

Outside of the gas chamber all the cadets were walking around spitting, slobbering, with mucus running from their eyes, nose and mouths profusely. The pain was unbearable, it felt as if a million red ants were biting you at once. It took about thirty minutes for the effects to subside. All protocol and ridicule went out the window during this thirty minutes though. People were cussing and crying, yelling and screaming. I had never experienced anything like this in my life and was kind of proud that I survived it and would be able to write home and tell people I went into a gas chamber.

Another favorite moment in Beast Barracks was when we hit the field with the exact orders to rappel down a seventy-five foot cliff. They taught us how to make Swiss seats, which were used for rappelling. This is the structure you would essentially rest your butt on and secure the rope with. It was sort of a figure eight that went around your legs and through your crotch. The only thing we cadets had to worry about was strategically placing the rope so we didn't singe our balls off. A properly constructed Swiss seat is essential to your manhood. Before it was our turn to rappel, we watched an awesome demonstration from the 10th Mountain Division in which they rappelled frontward and backwards. Some soldiers even had rappelled with another soldier on his back holding a rifle. This shit was fired up. I was excited, until I got my ass up on that 75-foot cliff.

Now the test run was a minor feat. It was about 20 feet high in the air. I attacked that twenty-foot cliff with no reservations. But our final test that would prove us proficient in rappelling was a mammoth of a cliff, standing 75 feet high in the air. They led us up this trail of tears to the point of no return. At the top of the cliff was this tall, blue eyed Captain that was stern in the voice and was not playing. When he ordered your ass to the starting point, you went, locked up and began to rappel down the cliff. At last is was my turn. I went up to the cliff, attached the rope to my Swiss seat and looked back over my shoulder. When I looked down, my whole outlook on rappelling and life changed. I saw cadets head over heels because they had let too much rope loose. I saw how damn far down it looked. I decided that shit wasn't for me. The Captain said, "Rappel Cadet". I looked at him with that look in my eye when I knew I wasn't going to do something. After a brief exchange of words, he ordered me to rappel at once. I obliged and took the leap of faith. All the training and the practice paid off. I made it to the bottom in about three or four bounds without falling. I felt extremely accomplished! This was yet another confidence builder in the midst of perseverance.

Long March Home

Even though I was a trained athlete, the physical training at West Point was rigorous. Every other day we had a morning run, then calisthenics. When we ran, we would sing cadences with passion. We would fall into formation and take off down and around West Point's beautiful campus. Everything was beautiful except the big, bold gray buildings. Running around the campus for what felt like forever. I was a track guy in high school and we used to run miles but damn, this seemed like we ran forever. It had to be at least 3 miles we ran every other day singing cadences with pride and fervor.

I have to say during those three mile runs the part that I grew to love and still cherish to this day were the cadences. Whoever invented cadences for marching and running were geniuses. My favorite cadence started out, "I wanna be an airborne ranger, live a life of guts and danger." It always got me pumped. "I wanna be a scuba diver, jump right in that murky water" was another line from that particular cadence that fired me up. When you feel all alone amidst a bunch of people that feel the same way it feels good to find something that bonds you all and puts you on level ground. These cadences took our minds off the grimy, hard but fair ways of basic training, and conditioned our minds to be proud and loyal soldiers of the United States Army.

The marches in full gear included ruck sacks filled to the brim with government issued essentials that were a must in the field. The ruck sack ended up weighing about 20 pounds. We were in full battle dress uniform, which included combat boots, BDU blouse and pant, equipment belt, and our glorious M16A2 assault rifles that we never in our lives let go of. Your weapon, in this case my M16A2 assault rifle, was your baby. You took your weapon everywhere you went, no matter what, it better be there on your shoulder or in your hand. If you were caught slipping without your weapon, an upper-classmen would steal your weapon to punish you.

Our first march was a light one-mile march that didn't really fade us because all the marching and drilling we did during the regular part of our day was probably equal to or greater than one mile. We were always drilling and marching to perfect our craft. What we didn't know was that they were setting us up on a series of marches in preparation for a grand finale. The next march would be a three-mile march that proved to be tougher. Your mind and body had to be disciplined. You had to make sure you were properly hydrated so that you didn't become a heat casualty or fall out of formation. The most embarrassing, unworthy situation during marches was to fall out of formation due to heat exhaustion, body failure or any other reason. It was a battle of the minds and body. No one wanted to be proved incapable. There was always a truck driving behind the whole formation to pick up people who had given up mentally or physically to carry them to the destination at hand. I told myself they would never have to pick me up. I had been through countless hell weeks and triple day practices, and I wasn't going to let a march defeat me.

Next was the five-mile march that tested us just a little bit more. Each march increased in both length and rigor. We marched through the woods and mountainous terrain, all while singing cadences over and over again. Whenever we heard the word halt, which rarely happened, we were so damn happy because it meant that we could finally rest, but not for long. When left to our own free will, people never push themselves this hard. We don't dare ourselves to greatness and find out what our minds and bodies can accomplish. These marches taught me that **there**

are a lot of things in life that can be accomplished if you only take the first step and keep going. You can only walk five miles if you walk the first five feet. One foot after the other, putting them down and picking them up, is what in the long run helps you accomplish your goals.

After eight weeks of being transitioned into a United States Military Academy cadet and active duty cadet of the United States Army, it was time for our most noteworthy task and test. It seemed as if other cadets knew this was about to happen, but I didn't. I was totally taken a back when I found out that our last march to prove our worthiness was going to be a thirteen mile march that would take all day. What I also didn't know is that traditionally, this is the time where parents come to visit and congratulate their cadets. Some cadets talked about their mothers or fathers or whole damn families for that matter coming to see them this weekend. I knew no one was coming to see me. All my folks lived in California, with the exception of my aunt who taught law in Harrisburg, Pennsylvania. She was the closest relative to me, but was probably in darkness about the whole situation.

The day came where the big hummers came to take us out into the field. We would stay there overnight, break camp in the morning, and march our asses all the way back through the West Point gates. We all loaded up in the trucks and set out for our camp ground which felt like it took forever to get to. I'm thinking in the back of my head how damn far we would have to be walking back without the aid of the hummers, strictly using our own two feet and a positive mental attitude. If you had a bad attitude, this march wasn't going to be for you. It was exciting at this point. We all knew the rules and what to do. It had become a beautiful thing. Thinking back to the first day when everyone was stuttering and tripping over their feet to now. Everyone had grown so much, and was ready to carry on with our mission.

We stayed in the field overnight, woke up that morning and broke camp. We packed up everything into our ruck sacks, got in formation and awaited the command. "Forward march." We took off, step for step, all you heard was boots hitting the ground and a call and response cadence. The beginning of the march was just like the others. We were used to this, this is what we did. We continued to march on and it seemed as if we marched with no clear end in sight. After a few hours and maybe one break the march began to seem unbearable. When we stopped at what appeared to be the West Point Golf Course to take a major break, it seemed as if we were over halfway done with the march. The look on cadet's faces was of dizziness, pure disgust and fatigue. At that point my body was on autopilot. We had been marching all day through and over rocks, dirt, hills and mountains. The never-ending journey was proving to be way more than never ending. It was like hell in a bottle. There was only one way to get back to the barracks and that was marching. So we marched on.

The last two or three miles proved to be a true test of my character, manhood and pride. At this point, the only thing that kept me going was pride. I had started out on this mission and I was sure that I was going to finish it. My body was telling me something else at this point. My feet hurt and I could feel the chaffing in my groin area from the battle dress trousers rubbing my inner thigh to the point where it felt like I had no skin left. Every single step came with pain. I was using every muscle in my body to keep my body going. I didn't know if I was going to pass out or die. What I did know is that the only way I didn't finish this march was if I passed out or died right there in formation.

I was beginning to have a bit of an outer-body experience. Hallucinations and odd figures started storming through my mind. At one point I swear I was standing outside my body watching myself march down the road. People and animals that weren't there were walking with me and sometimes speaking to me. I kept having to shake my head to rid myself of the ghost. I was being pushed to the absolute limit. No matter all the crazy hallucinations and thoughts that marched through my head, my feet kept moving one in front of the other. Indeed I started to reach my limit; I started to think about how I could get away with falling out of formation and riding back to the barracks in the hummer without embarrassing myself, my family, and the football team. But I couldn't, I had to ride this one out and persevere. So I did.

As we got closer, we started to see people along the sides of the road. They were there to cheer us on through the West Point gates. As we got closer to the gates parents had signs for their kids. Everyone on the side of the road looked so proud of us. We were beyond our limit of agony and pain. We were at the point of mental breakdown. We were at our breaking points. The sound of people's cheers and congratulatory phrases put a whole new life into us. We immediately stood straight up with strength. We marched on with zeal and purpose, putting on a show for the parents and families that lined up to encourage us. That last mile made me feel good. Drenched with sweat, I marched on to the end. I made it alive and was too tired to realize the significance of the journey.

The next day we graduated from Cadet Basic Training and were allowed to visit with our families and friends. I had been so lonely at West Point and desperately wanted to see my family. Despite all the joy that came with accomplishing a successful completion of basic training, I wasn't able to share it with the people I love. Back then, most of my family couldn't afford to fly from California to New York, and the others didn't realize how important their support would have been to my success. I just wished my parents or family were there to share this accomplishment with me.

Chapter 6

Army Football

With basic training over I now had bigger fish to fry –Army Football! Finally, the moment I'd been waiting my whole life for was finally here. It is what made me decide to join the academy. It was time for Army Football summer camp. This camp would last two weeks in which we would be surrounded by football. It would be a break from the regular happenings that was going on in regular cadet life but hard in itself. Even though there is always seniority and deference on football teams to the older players, it was still my happy place in which I could be myself and operate on more level grounds. I was excited for this moment and a bit nervous. A great showing in camp could land me on national television as a true freshmen. This was major. My goal was to travel with the team, suit up and start at strong safety.

We took over the sports complex adjacent to Michie Stadium. That was where we were going to be sleeping and eating. Although, there wasn't going to be much sleeping because the plan was to have a long morning practice, weights, films, another long ass practice, more meetings, a little bit of free time and then lights out. This was our schedule for the first two weeks, not including Sunday's, our day of rest. We were all issued a mattress to put on the floor and all the equipment we needed was in the locker room. The locker room is where we would shower and groom ourselves.

Among the college ranks of football the learning curve is expected to be fast. The practices were run at a fast pace even though they were long practices. Everything has a time limit and when the horn blows you better get with the program and get to the next station. At Army, and among other colleges and universities, self-policing is strong and in force among players. There were a few changes or tweaks to the coverage that Army ran, but most of it was really similar to my high school coverages. The terminology is what messed me up. There was a real disconnect with terminology with me when I got to college football.

On the field, however, I was representing, and doing well I thought. I was making tackles and not blowing coverages too often. I was in the first rotation, which was a sigh of relief. When you go to college everything is in black and white in your film rooms. After a little evaluation, a practice or two, there is a white board with names on it, then there's a big black horizontal line underneath those names with names below it. Your whole goal and duty as a football player is to keep your name above that line, and I was doing well keeping my name above that line.

The names above the line were people that would travel and suit up for games. The people at the top were starters. Indeed I wanted to start, but my goal was to be able to suit up, travel and play. I went out there everyday and practiced my heart out. The second week of practice would be our final evaluation. At the end of camp, my name was called. My defensive back coach, along with the running back coach, informed me that I would be switched to running back. It wasn't the position I expected, but I was determined to give it my all.

August 28, 1997

After camp, the academic school year at West Point began that following Monday. After a whole summer of marching, shooting, and being constructively hazed, it was time to start going to class and doing homework. We transitioned from our camp life at Michie Stadium back to our respective barracks where we would be for the remainder of the school year. I took classes in Pre-Calculus, World History, Chemistry, Physical Education, and English. So along with football, I would have a rigorous academic schedule. I was willing, and had no choice in the matter anyway.

This was an important week because not only

was school starting, but all the incoming freshmen class football players were scheduled to scrimmage the prep school. This was a traditional game that was played every year at the academy. I was fired up for this game. I would be starting running back in this game and would get to showcase my skills in front of all the coaches and onlookers. Fired up and ready to go. The game was on Thursday, August 28th, 1997 in Michie Stadium. This was the precursor to the season opener against Marshall University on September 6th. Marshall had an awesome receiver that all the upper class defensive backs were talking about.

We practiced all week leading up to Thursday. During which we practiced singing the Alma Mater because singing the Alma Mater after football games was another Army Football tradition. This school was based off tradition. After being there for so many weeks, all the traditions and legends started to get internalized, including famous quotes. One of my favorite West Point quotes is from General Douglas MacArthur:

"Upon the fields of friendly strife, are sown the seeds, that upon other fields, on other days, will bear the fruits of victory."

Finally the game came. I remember meeting in the team room, fully padded, bearing the number 42. I was ready to go and at this point still didn't know all the terminology for the offense but I understood at least what I was supposed to do for basic plays. I had only been a running back for a week up to this point. We rallied the troops, coaches made the hype speeches and we took the field.

This being a game for freshmen only, it wasn't a true big deal to the uninitiated, but to the Army staff and the freshmen football players this was the place to be. In the huddle, the quarterback called '22 counter'. This was my play. My stomach immediately tightened up; sweat dripping from my facemask and a few butterflies in my stomach. But with great confidence I smiled and nodded. It doesn't get any better than this. Hearing your number called in the huddle is equivalent to winning the lottery. I took a deep breath as we broke the huddle, and was ready to go as the quarterback started the cadence. Ready, set, go!

I counter stepped to the left with a shoulder and head fake to go with it. I bucket stepped back to the right to go get the football. The quarterback was reverse pivoting around and our eyes never met as I came around and took the hand off. Just as I approached the end of the line near the offensive tackle a defender approached. Someone had missed their block but it didn't matter because I side-stepped him with an old school shake. As I shook him and hit the corner, there was no one in sight. I was gone. I rolled down the sideline huffing and puffing trying to get to the end zone. Down field I approached my wide receiver and the defensive back from the prep school. I was on the sideline. The wide receiver had fallen down trying to stock block for me. The defensive back was getting up. I had to make a decision. Do I step out of bounds, or show this defensive back what I'm made of? I chose the latter. As I stayed in bounds and lowered my pads, the defensive back lowered his pads too. There was no way I was going to run out of bounds. My pride and ego was telling me to run this guy over and go get that touchdown. It was more instinct than self-dialogue, but that was the decision I made nevertheless. I was taking a step with my left leg in the turf when we collided. I blacked out.

A few seconds later I remember coming to in pain. I couldn't get up. It was my knee. I remember lying on that astro turf with tears in my eyes, pain stemming from my knee and my surrounding muscles. I didn't know what was wrong but I knew it had to be a bad situation the way all the coaches and trainers ran onto the field. They all saw what happened to me, and they said it looked pretty bad. All I remember is being carted off the field in agony, and waking up in the West Point hospital.

When I moved to run that other player over, he apparently got lower than me and went to take my knee out. This could have all been avoided if I stepped out of bounds, I thought. To this day I wonder what would have happened if I stepped out of bounds. Anyway, when he hit my knee dead center, my foot was stuck in the astro turf. Astro turf of the 80s and 90s had no give. Many a football players ended their careers in the same way. When my foot didn't give there was nothing for my knee to do but give itself. My knee suffered a major hyperextension. My knee bent backwards, the wrong way, caused by the force of the blow. The doctor said that I was lucky my entire knee wasn't dislocated, which would have happened if the defensive back weighed a little more.

Afterwards, my coach came in the hospital room to speak with me. With a solemn look on his face he tried to keep the mood positive he said, "That was a great run. This injury is bad but not that bad, you will be able to rehab and be ready for next spring. You're going to be our guy." When you're lying in a hospital bed in August, and someone is telling you about how you're going to be in the Spring, it doesn't quite help your morale as much as they probably think it does.

This was the most painful injury I had ever experienced. With the exception of a few pulled muscles and a concussion, I had never been injured in my career. I made it through high school not having missed a game or practice. I couldn't walk without the aid of crutches, couldn't put any pressure on my left leg, and had to get an MRI done. The MRI results showed that I had a partial tear in my posterior capsular ligament. The good news was that it was only a partial tear and the bad news was that it could take up to ten weeks to rehab if I worked hard. I talked to my mother and my father via phone call and they just offered words of encouragement that went in one ear and out the other. It seems like you can hold yourself together until you hear the voice of your mother. I broke down crying. My morale was at a normal low for a player that just ended his season, but over the course of the next few weeks it became worse.

Rehab

With the hope of making it back before the season ended, I set my sights on rehabbing my knee and getting it back right. In the meantime, real academy life was in full effect. School was strenuous, rigorous at the least. All my classes had homework every single night. I had multiple papers being assigned from my World History and English classes. All these assignments were taking their toll on my mental capacity, and stressing me out. Something had to give. I was hobbling around West Point on crutches. It is a rule at West Point that cadets can't carry backpacks. So I was getting around with a broken wheel, using crutches and carrying all my books at the same time. The gray buildings and gray uniforms started to symbolize depression; I was losing my mind.

I was going to rehab every day. Sitting in the

ice bath up to my waist. You would think it was unbearable but after a while you got used to it. Those first few minutes though, when you emerge yourself beneath the waterline was like a cold hell. Very ironic, but that's the best way to describe it. My knee looked like a soccer ball for a couple weeks. The swelling and pain eventually went down a little bit but my knee would still buckle when pressure was put on it.

Rehab became part of my everyday life— I was either at class or at rehab. My morale, however, continued to decrease, and my positive mindset was totally gone. I wasn't able to do what I love, which was play football. I was never happy and started caring less and less about important things such as academics and hygiene. In the evenings I wouldn't do any homework after rehab because I was so depressed. I would get up late in the mornings, roll out the bed and hobble down to formation with no shower. I was a complete mess. And every time I talked to my family I would break down crying.

I would go days wearing the same uniform, just waking up, putting on my stuff and going about my business. All the clothes in the locker room were washed together, jock straps, shorts, and socks. I believe this practice along with my lack of personal hygiene is what caused a rash on my inner thigh. Everything was going wrong all at once. It was all sending me down into a deeper depression. I don't remember anyone at the academy ever asking me how I was doing or noticing any signs of depression. I just felt like I was completely on my own.

Gray is a common theme at West Point. The long gray line. All the buildings are gray in color, with a gothic look. Most of the uniforms are gray. In the fall and winter, the sky is gray. When you're depressed, this gray sends your moods into a gray place. A place where you don't care about anything that you would usually care about. I was starting to contemplate ways I could get out of the academy. I thought about doing something wrong where they would have to kick me out of the academy. I thought about failing out so they would have to send me home. My joy and passion for football was starting to fade. I was transforming into a totally different person. It all originated from one decision to run someone over instead of step out of bounds. That play kept replaying in my head.

As a depressed cadet, I didn't care about the rules of the academy. I started getting written up for belligerence and being out of order, and I would talk back with an attitude. My behavior got me in front of the Captain who over saw our company on a couple different occasions. One particular time she informed me that I was failing all of my classes. This was a bombshell because I hadn't even thought about grades. This was about six weeks into the semester. She told me that at the rate I was going, I wouldn't be able to play football in the spring. So, I decided to put more effort into my studies and did so.

One weekend we had leave and since I was not traveling with the football team I decided to go visit my aunt in Harrisburg. I had to be issued a wheel chair in the airport because I was on crutches. An attendant helped me get from gate to gate. I had a great time with my aunt and her family, but the reality was I had to go back to what I saw as a gray place of darkness. Football was becoming less desirable; my emotions were making me a walking time bomb, and nothing mattered anymore.

The football team wasn't doing too well either. I would be in the stands instead of the sidelines at home games. My dreams of playing on Saturdays got crushed by my injury. Instead of taking handoffs from the quarterback, I would be in the stands with the other players that weren't suited up listening to the student body scream, "Rock the Black Gold," or "USMA Rah Rah." I so desired to be on the field. After the games, cadet's parents and families that tailgated would give us food and drink. A lot of cats from the East Coast had parent representation at the games, and I had no one. No one ever came from California to visit me. I was walking around with the aide of crutches, no family, and a wrecked mindset. Shattered dreams and a broken heart ruled my life at this point.

I was depressed, but the little pride I still had told me that I couldn't quit the football team. I had to persevere and not quit on my squad. I knew for sure I wouldn't quit. Then, I got a call from my mother and she informed me that she would be visiting my aunt and it would be a good idea for me to go back to Harrisburg so she could see me. She was excited and missed me. I told her I would fly out there since I wouldn't be traveling with the team anyway. This meeting would prove to be my breaking point.

When I got off the plane in Harrisburg, I saw my mother and aunt and the rest of the family. I was in my dress uniform that we traveled in. They all thought I was so honorable. Later that evening, my mother and I went outside to take a walk and talk. This was when I broke down –tears flowed from my eyes like a river. My mother shed tears for her broken hearted son at the same time. It was a turning point. I was at a low. There I was, a grown man, 18 years of age, been through basic training and was a football player on a Division I team, and there I was crying in full force on my mother's shoulder. I knew exactly how it felt to hit rock bottom.

Scout Team

Despite my depression, I was able to rehab my knee back and join the team again. I wasn't one hundred percent but I was about 75 percent full speed. Being at practice instead of rehab brought some joy to my heart. However, it was so late into the season, already November, I was headed straight to the offensive scout team. It was too late for the coaches to try and work me in. Plus I was told that I could use that season as a medical red shirt year and it wouldn't count against my eligibility.

The game against Air Force was on that first Saturday after I had returned to the team. I was starting on the scout team, and started to realize the love and respect the scout team players deserved. You go out there every day, with no hopes of getting into the game or suiting up just for the good of the team. For the betterment of the program, you go out there and bust your ass. No glory, but lots of guts. Our head coach understood how important a hard working scout team was so he had a recognition system in place in which he honored scout team players for their hard work in preparation for a game.

Even though I wasn't one hundred percent as far as speed, I was still able to show out a little bit. My job was to make the defense look bad. It was a fun job, but came with its disadvantages as well. Whenever you made the defense look bad, the coach would cuss that person you made look bad out as well as the whole defense and make them run the play again. In one situation on a swing pass to the right, the defensive back came up and I shook him so bad and spun out of his grasp. The whistle immediately blew... "Run it again," which were the words an offensive scout team player hated to hear. Now we would be running the same exact play, and the defense would be ready for it. We ran it again, the same defensive back came up and smashed me. That's the life you live on scout team.

The following Monday, the head coach showed me love in the team meeting and announced that I and some other scout team players were Army Football Rangers for that previous week leading up to the Air Force game. We didn't beat Air Force that season, but that week has forever stayed in my heart because of the honor of making the Ranger list. North Texas, Boston College and Navy were all left on the schedule. I would have an important role in the preparation for these games as well. I made the ranger list for Boston College week as well. The Army-Navy game would be December 6th, 1997 at the Meadowlands Sports Complex in East Rutherford New Jersey.

Beat Navy week was ridiculous. Everyone at West Point was fired up. All the plebes are walking around greeting the upper classmen with the phrase "Beat Navy." The whole student body was chartered to New Jersey and put in hotels for the night to attend the game. This was a break from the normal events of the academy. We were able to hang out in New Jersey for a night, attend the game the next day and breathe a little easier than normal. The stadium was packed with alumni from both academies and thousands of servicemen and women. It is truly a remarkable event to be a part of. This would wrap up a long football season, and a series of life changing events for me. Despite the good time, Navy beat us 39-7.

"Hope never abandons you, you abandon it."
-unknown

Chapter 7

Going Back to Cali

During the last few weeks of the football season a depression had set in that was hard to shake. The thing that I loved to do most in my entire life, and the root of all of my dreams, had become a burden and unworthy of my passion. Football became a burden because I felt it was keeping me in a place I didn't want to be, and was the cause of my anguish. My whole life's ambition and fuel had ran out. Hit with a hard blow from reality, I made a very emotional decision to leave the United States Military Academy and never play football again. Luckily, I was smart enough and had enough sense not to give up my education as a whole but my young eighteen year old mind told me that my dream was over. I rationalized it in my own head by saying to myself that at least I made it to a Division I school and was able to experience a season. Yet and still, my overall goal of starting, and playing on Saturday mornings in front of a roaring crowd would be lost forever.

One mistake I made was that I never sought guidance about my decision. By the time I decided to announce my departure, it was basically too late for anyone to talk me out of it. My mind was made up. I had already sent out applications to attend Cal States in the spring and was accepted by all the schools that I sent applications off too. I couldn't go to Cal Berkeley because it was a UC school, and if you don't enter as an incoming freshman, you have to wait until you're a 60-credit transfer student. So, emotionally distraught, and still depressed, I still managed to put a plan together that wouldn't leave me back home and out of school. For the sake of my ego, I decided I would be in California, but far from home if I chose to go to a Cal State school.

I remember writing my high school coach, who played a very important role in getting me to West Point in the first place, to tell him that I was leaving West Point and I wouldn't be playing football anymore. A couple days later I received a four-page letter from my coach full of encouraging words. He said in one part of the letter, "You're making an emotional decision, get it together and I'll see you in four years at your graduation." At that point I didn't know that he was right because I was too emotional. He was right, but it took me years to realize it. At that very moment, I thought I was making a good decision. I packed his letter away and still decided to announce my departure.

When I announced my departure to the coaches they were shocked. Mainly shocked because despite my injury, I had persevered the whole season and came back to make a positive impact on the scout team. They had no idea I was depressed and unhappy. But they hadn't asked me how I was doing either. I don't remember anyone at West Point that had an authoritative role or mentor role ever ask me how I was doing or how my morale was. It seemed as if so much was going on, I just fell through the cracks. Or maybe they couldn't detect it. When I told my coach I was leaving he tried to convince me to stay, but very soon realized that my mind was already made up.

He asked me what my plan was and I told him that I had applied to some Cal State Universities, and I would choose one that had a football team. In his final attempt to show some care he asked if I wanted him to make a phone call to those football programs on my behalf and let them know I may be coming. Depressed and fed up, I told him no. But then he said something to me that I have never forgotten. He said, "You're going to regret this in five years." It scared me. I promised myself that I would never regret it.

My next step was letting my chain of command know that I was getting out of there. It hurt me so much to leave the football team. They were the only program in the country that believed in me enough to offer me a scholarship, I felt really bad to turn my back on the team. The academy on the other hand, not so much. I enjoyed being a soldier, and all the necessary things I learned during basic training, but without football, I would have never ended up there in the first place. I wouldn't miss the academy life, only the football life.

It wasn't easy however, leaving the academy. When a cadet wants to leave there is a formal process that has to be followed. You have to take part in three different counseling sessions to make sure you really want to leave. After that you have to do exit interviews with the West Point doctor and dentist. When all the paperwork was signed, and they gave me pins to recognize that I was no longer a plebe, it was then over. When I finished the whole process and was ready to go, there was still about a week and a half left in the semester before I was to leave.

Before leaving West Point, while I was at the eating table with the team, a teammate at the head of the table called me out about leaving the academy. His words to me were: "Get the f**k off our football tables! You're no longer a part of our brotherhood, so go eat somewhere else." He said it with fire in his eyes. I was crushed because I thought the football team was my family. I tried to hold back the tears with pride as I got up from the table, turned away and left. That's when the tears started flowing. In a matter of months my life had turned into shambles, and I was hurting inside worse than I had ever hurt before.

When the day finally came for me to depart

West Point the Army issued me a ticket to get me back home and I would be flying into Ontario International Airport. All my personal belongings had been shipped home via USPS. I sold all my uniforms back to the Academy with the exception of my battle dress uniforms and my combat boots that I loved so much. As I left, I rode through the West Point grounds reflecting on what I had been through over the last six months, and all the good and rough times. As I closed my eyes a tear simultaneously rolled down my cheek as the shuttle rolled through the West Point gates. I was leaving a part of me at the academy. A part of my heart that motivated me to do well in school and life. A burning desire and ambition to play football was left at the academy, perhaps right on the twenty yard line of Michie Stadium where my dreams came crashing to a screeching halt.

San Jose State

When my flight landed in Ontario from West Point, I was greeted by my mother and my sister, who was home on Christmas break. I remember getting off the plane and seeing their faces. I hadn't seen my mother since we were at my aunt's house during the football season, and I hadn't seen my sister in about six months. I missed seeing them. When they greeted me they could see that I was different –unhappy and not my usual self. But they could also sense from me that I was happy to be home. I spent some time visiting everyone, including my brothers and my uncle, who had spent some time in the Air Force during the end of the Vietnam War. He said I looked different and had changed. We talked for a while about basic training and other things.

I made the decision to go to San Jose State University instead of Fresno State or San Diego State. I thought San Diego and Fresno were cool schools, but what inspired me to go to San Jose was a song. The famous rapper from Oakland had a line in an older song that said: *I was on my way, to San Jose, 'cause one amp shut down and my music won't play.* This line always stuck in my head. When it was time for me to make my decision, I chose San Jose State for that very reason, and the fact that my sister was attending Stanford University, which was not too far away. I had never been to San Jose State to visit, although I had flown into the airport my senior year in high school to visit my sister at Stanford. I was excited to start a new life, yet still feeling a little depressed.

Classes at San Jose State started on January 20th, 1998. I flew into San Jose on a Sunday night, my sister and her homeboy, who later became a good friend of mine as well, picked me up and drove me to the campus. Wearing my Army field jacket, combat boots and some blue jeans, I checked in with the Residential Director and moved in. I must say though that I was still in West Point mode. I came with one bag, and a clothes hamper full of stuff, mostly blankets. I still had the government issued pillow from West Point and my USMA blanket. I immediately made up my bed West Point style. Hospital corners on the bed. Nothing on the desk or walls, as I was used to this protocol from being at the academy. The academy had thoroughly brainwashed (or trained) me. I didn't even realize it until I tried to mix with regular civilians.

I was assigned to Hoover Hall. Hoover Hall was one of the six brick residence halls at San Jose State. It was right on campus and close to everything. My roommate was a Latino dude from Los Angeles. His side of the room had all kinds of pictures, while my side of the room was bare and simply a place to sleep. I started to meet many people on campus – some of whom I knew from high school in Southern California. I started to make some real friends.

To my surprise, one day I met some of the football players and realized that I knew some of them from high school. A cat that played for Rancho Cucamonga High School, that led the area, county, and state in Touchdowns in 1996 was now at San Jose State. It turns out that he was prop 48'd and was doing well there. A quarterback that was now playing defensive end from San Gorgonio High School was also there. He had played with my cousin at San G, class of 1994. All the football players seemed cool, but I had no interest in playing. Our mutual interest in the game kept us friends.

San Jose State was a very diverse campus. One aspect that I was interested in was the Black Greek letter organizations. I immediately set out to find out the scoop about the Omegas. My brother told me before I left home that there was a chapter on the yard at San Jose, but I would have to seek out the brothers and let them know I was interested. And that's exactly what I did. Springtime is usually pledging season at most universities. Word had got out that the Alphas were going to have a probate show, where the incoming members do steps and recite information. I was excited about the whole fraternity scene and decided that it would be cool to attend this event. When I got there, I was shocked that the entire Black community at the school was in attendance. This was clearly a major event. The Black Greeks on campus were looked up to and pretty much ran all the events outside of the Black Student Union. This was something I wanted to be a part of.

Having moved around my whole life from school to school, and city to city, I wasn't afraid of new places or new things. My transition to San Jose was pretty smooth. During that spring semester of 1998 I showed some signs of depression due to the injury and football not working out, although I was healing. The after effects of West Point were still ingrained in me as I was still a little rigid and programmed from academy living. I was still a little anti-social from my depression and it showed. I did however, try my luck with the ladies. My swag was not up though I must say but I was known because of my job inside the cafeteria's Jamba Juice. The ladies didn't really show me any love that semester. That in itself was kind of depressing. I had to get my swag back.

One thing I did continue to do when I got to San Jose State was lift weights. I saved all the Creatine that I was supposed to be taking at Army, and started using it once I got to San Jose. I was getting bigger and stronger and it was helping me get my confidence back.

Nonetheless, it took me a whole semester to climb myself out of that depression that started way back in September of 1997 when I was at the academy. It had almost been a whole year and remnants of the depression were still lingering. My only problem is I didn't know what was wrong with me. Who'd have thought that I would go from high school hero to zero.

Home for Summer 1998

San Jose State gets out of school for the Summer break on Memorial Day weekend. Right around this time, every year since 1992, my brother's fraternity had been throwing Omega Fest at Cal State

San Bernardino and UC Riverside. This was the event of the summer and sometimes the year. His frat brothers would come from all over the country to participate in this three day fest. Friday night was a pajama/lingerie party, Saturday was a pool party, and Sunday was always a toga party. This event is what initially opened my eyes to his fraternity and their traditions such as gold boots with purple laces, camouflage pants and their hardcore stepping, they called marching. I was very happy to start my vacation off in this manner. Hanging out with my brother and being around other college students from around the state and country. It was a good time.

The Omega Fest was a stone cold groove. Thousands of people would come to watch the brothers do what they called marching and hopping. Traditional stepping has dated back many years. Time would stop for them as they did their thing. Everything inside of me wanted to be a part of that history, legacy and brotherhood.

The summer of 1998 I set out for a summer job with the temporary work companies. Temp companies were popular back then. I had low skills, so the only jobs I would get were for little pay. They started me out at $6/hour. That means if I worked an eight-hour shift, minus lunch, I would make $42 dollars per day. Even in 1997 $42 dollars a day was low. I stacked salt, and I bottled rubbing alcohol and other things in warehouses close to Cal State San Bernardino for two weeks. At the end of the week, I would wake up exhausted and with very little money. There had to be a better way.

That's when I teamed up with a childhood friend that I was very close to and we decided that we were going to hustle trees over the summer to make some extra money. Yes, I became the weed man. I could make way more money selling trees in one hour than I could working in that warehouse.

That first day we drove around to all the people we knew smoked weed and let them know we were in business. Most people weren't really interested, but said they would take our numbers. I was on my way to go buy a pager so I just gave them the house phone number. It moved really slow the first week. Nothing really big happened other than selling some dimes and nicks to a few cats. The ounce was almost gone, I had paid $50 dollars for it. The first fifty bucks that I made back I put away. I was glad to see that the rest of the money I could do whatever I wanted with.

I put my first three hundred dollars aside and watched my pockets grow ever increasingly over the next few weeks. I never went back to the salt mill again. My mother asked me why I hadn't been going to work and I just told her I didn't like the job. She had no idea what I was really doing. I got up every day waiting for my pager to go off and my main focus was trying to keep the weed smell at a minimum so my cover wouldn't be blown. With all of the money I was making, I was able to buy groceries for my mom, help her with some bills and still party and hit Club Metro whenever I wanted. This would be the beginning of my addiction to fast money.

The Fraternity World

Summer ended and it was time for me to get back to San Jose. I was eager to get back, mostly because I wanted to do everything I could to be down with Greek life and pledge Omega. When you're interested in a Black Greek letter organization, especially Omega, you have to seek them out because they don't recruit. I knew this so every chance I got I was trying to introduce myself and become known.

Some of my homeboys from the dorms had just crossed Sigma and were sporting their letters around campus. There were some Deltas who had just crossed in the spring that were out and representing as well. This was making me even more excited, dreaming of the day I could wear those purple and gold letters like my brother. I met up with an older brother along with about four other guys that were interested to talk about his plans to bring the chapter back. He talked about community service like Toys for Tots and other honorable programs. He wanted to incorporate the mandated programs of the fraternity into the yearly accomplishments of the chapter. His goal was to take care of business and not just party. This sounded good to me, and he had my attention. With my focus on being a fraternity man, the hurt of my past seemed to take a back seat. It goes to show you that **when you set positive goals, and actively pursue them, even your failures become a blur**.

That whole semester I spent most of my time getting to know other brothers within the fraternity and learning the history of the Xi Gamma chapter, which is the chapter on San Jose State's campus. We talked to several professional gentlemen that had come through the chapter and were now very established in their respective communities. Some of them lived in the Bay Area, and others had moved on to other places. One brother was the president of a medical college, another notable brother was a District Attorney in Los Angeles. This chapter had a rich history and was full of men of great character. This was an organization I knew I needed to be a part of. Being associated with the brothers gave me a sense of pride, similar to being a part of a football team.

The old school brothers of the chapter set up an official interest meeting, in which we helped pass out fliers to the other Black males on campus to invite them to learn more about this glorious fraternity that we were seeking to get into. The interest meeting was carried out with a lot of passion and enthusiasm from the brothers. They spoke about their fraternity with the utmost respect and nobility. There were a bunch of brothers there but only a few of us were in the audience. The audience was made up of myself and about five other gentlemen. The speaker that night had been working for Omega for almost twenty years. He was so fired up that he started marching and chanting. I was sitting in the front row on the edge of my seat. This was definitely what I wanted to be a part of.

That whole semester, if I wasn't working I was probably doing something with the brothers helping out at a function or volunteering for an event. We were getting to know the brothers really well, but there was always people you didn't know. The fraternity was big. The old school brothers told us that we had to meet everyone and get to know them, to make sure the fraternity was really what we wanted. So we spent most of our spare time riding around with him just meeting folks and learning the culture of the fraternity. We went on the website and started learning different important dates and some of the history of the fraternity. We were excited to do this because it meant we were getting one step closer.

1999

It was a new year and I was excited to get back to campus. After going home for a week or two over the winter, I came back to school early to find out I wouldn't have a job at the grill anymore. I saw my friend walking on campus and asked her where she was going, she told me she was going to work. After a short conversation about how I didn't have a job, she invited me to talk with her supervisor because they were looking for someone as soon as possible to hire. She worked at the telecommunications center on campus, the place that directed all the incoming calls. Her supervisor hired me on the spot.

Things were beginning to move forward for us to join the fraternity. Only two of us would be taking the journey. However, before we could be welcomed in, there were important things we first had to know and do. We learned manhood, taking care of our responsibilities in life, the importance of Scholarship, to never stop learning and to take pride in our education. We also learned that perseverance was key, and it was the answer to the hardships of life. We were taught to always uplift and encourage our brothers and friends when they are down or in need. After several weeks of seeking knowledge it was all coming to an end, but not before we were informed that it was our turn to show off everything we learned in the form of a probate show just as I had witnessed others perform in the past. I was excited to be showcased in front of the entire Black Greek community, but nervous at the same time. This was the moment of truth.

Our assignment was to march in front of Joe West Hall where the entire student body would be and recite all the information that we learned in front of this crowd. Probate shows are platforms for the little brothers to show off all the hard work and dedication they had committed to while proving themselves worthy of initiation. I was excited because my brother flew in from San Bernardino as a surprise to see me. It was a Friday, March 5th, 1999 when we jumped out the van at Williams street and 9th avenue and started marching down the street. Crouched real low, with grit and enthusiasm, sweat dripping from our noses all you could hear was our boots stomping the ground in unison and the loud chant we were singing "Zoom, zoom," all the way to Joe West Hall where this massive crowd awaited and looked on. Different people from all the local campuses, mainly other Greeks and Black folks, came to see us represent our struggle and journey.

Dressed in camouflage field jackets, black beanie caps, dark shades, black pants with a sewn on purple stripe and the oh so glorious jungle boots spray painted metallic gold, we marched up to the steps of Joe West and started our show. I was the head, the Ace, so everything went on my command.

"Dog team," you heard being yelled throughout the show. We recited all of our information including poems that had been internalized by then and meant so much to us, and we also greeted the brothers and paid our respects to other organizations as well. After reciting our information with pride and precision, we set out our hop show, traditional steps and corresponding chants. Through the dark shades, and the darkness of the night, all I could see were the silhouettes of different people clapping, yelling, screaming, and barking. The crowd was going crazy. It was a night to remember.

This was it, finally it. On that night, March 5th, 1999, I was initiated into the most glorious fraternity of them all. The Omega Psi Phi Fraternity, Incorporated, Xi Gamma chapter. I was born to be an Omega man, and with some hard work it manifested. This would change my life forever.

Homeless

While spending all my time working for Omega, I missed an important piece of mail that came to my apartment. The Housing office that controlled the dorms sent me a form that I was to sign and send back stating that I would be back in Spartan Village for the Fall semester of 1999. Of course I never saw this paper until it was too late. It must have fallen through the cracks. However, I did receive the piece of mail stating I had to be out of my apartment by June 24th when the person who takes over my room moves in.

After being fired from the telecommunications job for taking frequent naps while pledging, a friend hooked me up with a job at the airport renting cars for Alamo Rent-a-Car. I decided I would be able to handle not having a place to live for a couple months and it would actually save me some money on rent. I decided to just live out of my car and between friends' houses.

My homeboy, who's the reason that I got the job at Alamo, was also homeless and we teamed up to try different ways to obtain shelter. We would shack up at different friend's houses or be up all night somewhere just hanging out until we found an outlet. Eventually we realized that it was too hard to be homeless as a group, always looking for a corner to sleep in. He ended up staying in Moulder Hall with a friend, while I traveled all around the Bay area staying with frat brothers, my sister at Stanford, or a young lady I was talking to in Hayward.

For the first couple weeks this lifestyle was fun and adventurous, but when school started and classes began, it was hard to continue to live like a vagabond. I was so used to driving around from San Jose to Sacramento, or Oakland to Chico, San Francisco to Stanford, I found that I couldn't settle down. I was working full time, and had nowhere to study.

Since I lived in my car, I was always in my car. I would often be pulling in to work coming from where ever I was the night before. Often getting there a little early so I could pull off some sleep in the parking lot. One night, after a Xi Gamma reunion, I was hit from behind going east on the 580 freeway in East Oakland getting ready to get off at Edwards. My dean and I ended up almost going off a cliff before being stopped by the side railing on the highway. Needless to say I took everything out of my car and left the car on the side of the road in Oakland. It wouldn't have been so bad if I wasn't living out of my car. I had to store some of my belongings at his house until I could find another car.

My luck with cars kept going south. After wrecking my Regal while I was working for Omega, I got a '82 Tercel that gave me problems over and over again. First it was the axel breaking, then it was broken into and my things were scattered on the street. This was perhaps the worst part of living out of your car, because all your personal things were at the mercy of crack heads, thieves and robbers. This was my lifestyle for six months.

Things did get better though. I was able to find a room in a Victorian style house a block away from campus on 6th and Williams Street. I moved in quickly. This proved to be a blessing because the rigors of being homeless, and not knowing where you're going to sleep at night was getting to be too much. Being homeless had an adverse effect on my stress level and studies because my life was too unpredictable. I never knew when or where I was going to go to sleep, shower, eat or stay for the night. Sometimes I slept in my car. All this spontaneity was too much for me to settle down and try and study somewhere, so I just ignored my school work. Which wasn't a great decision even though I didn't think about it at the time.

My driving situation and my living situation became a lot better but that didn't make up for the lack of scholarship. Being homeless, and living the fast life had taken its toll and I failed every single class that semester. By now I had changed my major from Political Science to Marketing, the classes were full, the major was compacted and the professors were tough. They were trying to weed out the weak every chance they got. I decided that I would do better now that I had a room and somewhere to sleep and study. I reasoned with the counselor stating that the only reason I failed every class was because of being homeless. They gave me a break, let me stay in school and remain in the marketing program without being placed on academic probation. I was grateful I had another chance.

Chapter 8

Loss of Focus

My entire life I grew up with a dream. However, I had reached a point in my life where I no longer had a dream. It was nobody else's fault but my own. I decided to leave the academy and to never play football again. As a result, I was deferring my own dream. **When a man is living every day without a dream, he is most likely going nowhere.** After leaving the academy, the mistake that I made was not creating another dream for myself, another passion that was supported by smaller goals. If I had done this, there is no way I would have been failing out of school. So I went on through life, living day to day, just going through the motions. These motions turned out to have bitter consequences.

After I was blessed with the room on 6th and Williams, and vowed to the counselor that I would change my ways, I didn't. With no goal or end in sight, I was simply out there. I was lost, subconsciously seeking high self-esteem. There were things that I concentrated on with passion like my fraternity, my job at Alamo, selling weed, and throwing parties. Selling bomb weed and throwing parties made up my primary focus. The fast money, reputation and superstar status became addictive. Being a respected hustler with fast money and women replaced the void of being a scholarship athlete. Unfortunately, school and my studies was not on my to-do list. The irony to this is that the fraternity's cardinal principle of scholarship was being neglected even though I was so actively involved.

During the Spring Semester of 2000, while pledging the *"Two Shady Dogs,"* I seemed to have worn out my welcome on 6th Street. Occasional parties, my music, the traffic from weed exchanges and just being a wild college student forced the house to vote me out. I was being evicted. I received a thirty-day notice and went right to work locating somewhere to stay. There was no way in hell that I was going to be homeless again. I persevered and made it through the first time, but there would not be a second time if I could help it. Plus, at this point I was moving weight consistently and needed a stable, safe spot to keep my bounty and trees safe.

My Nigerian homeboy had just moved into some studios on 9th and Williams Street and told me the adjoining roommate had just moved out. He introduced me to his landlord and he said I could move in. I set up shop in this studio, still a block from campus so the money was still flowing. I was still working at Alamo and taking a full load of classes. During the last year or so, drinking had become an ever-increasing part of my life. I remember walking through campus on the way to class with a 22-ounce bottle of designer beer in a brown bag every day.

From throwing parties to attending different events or just chilling, getting drunk, women and making fast money became my addiction.

What do washed up athletes do when the thrill is gone? I don't know, but I know what made me feel like a star again and that was walking around with fat pockets. When you're serving on campus, everyone knows who you are and you can pretty much do or buy whatever you like. I wasn't the star football player anymore; people didn't even know I played football. What people did know was that I was the cool dude with the trees that threw big parties. I had transformed my whole disposition from jock to hustler. I was getting as much attention on campus as the football players on scholarship. Sometimes the football players were jealous of me. The reputation became a need and I was fulfilling that need the best I could. All of a sudden I knew all the people that had the drugs on campus –all the strippers, all the shady cats that had the stolen merchandise, and everyone that lived fast. The funny thing about it is that we were all in college. We were trying to get paid, and it was easy when everyone lived right on campus. College turned out to be a money pot instead of an institution of higher learning.

I started to concentrate more on money and having fun and less and less on my studies. I would be all over the bay area and you could often find me at a lady friend's house instead of the library. With tons of traffic coming to my studio, and my pager going off constantly, I was not focused on school at all. I was put on academic probation and taken off financial aid. One semester the school called me and said I would have to pay my tuition for that semester because financial aid was no longer going to be provided to me because of grades. Without flinching, I counted out over a thousand dollars and walked to admissions to pay the bill. I still ended up failing every class that semester and wasting my money.

In the Spring of 2001, while my good 2001 lone dog was working for Omega and Xi Gamma, I had a talk with the counselors once again. They were tired of the sob stories that I always seemed to come up with. Bottom line was that if my grades weren't up at the end of the semester, San Jose State would be a thing of my past. I understood, but it didn't seem to register. It was too late into the semester anyway. I knew for sure I couldn't make up all the assignments and work that I had already missed. It was pretty much a wrap and I knew it.

After throwing a huge party in the student union that May things made a turn for the worse. Brothers had come from all around, from 2000 Zeta Mu (Dominguez Hills), '96 Pi Mu (San Diego), Sigma Eta (Cal State/UCR), '98 Epsilon Mu (Berkeley), Pi Chi (San Francisco) and Iota Mu (Chico/Davis/Sac). All these men in a little studio, you can imagine the chaos. The climax of the whole weekend is when I

180

was embarrassed by my landlord. He kicked in my door as we were hopping around, drinking and chanting and told me I had to get my crazy friends out of his building. As I got all of them out of the studio I went to the phone booth at the neighborhood gas station to make a call. That's when I was approached and handcuffed by the San Jose Police Department. How was I supposed to know the gas station had just been broken into? The police detained me for almost an hour waiting for the owner to come review the video. After the police reviewed the video, they let me out of the patrol car. I was evicted from my studio that following Tuesday. Another thirty-day notice. Shortly thereafter, I was informed that I wouldn't be coming back to San Jose State. IT WAS ALL OVER.

Oakland, CA

After moving in for about a month or so with my frat brother that actually graduated from West Point, ironic as it sounds, I actually moved out of San Jose to Oakland with two of my frat brothers. The advisors at San Jose State told me that if I wanted to get back into San Jose State and graduate, I would have to take a program of study for a semester and come back with nothing less than a "B" average in two classes. Living in Oakland now, I decided to go to Laney College, which is located near downtown Oakland.

This same summer, my mother graduated from Cal State San Bernardino with her bachelor's degree. She had returned to school when I graduated high school. I arrived at West Point as part of the class of 2001, and here it was 2001 and I had only completed about 40 units, I knew it was time to focus. Playtime was over. I went to Laney College and enrolled in a couple Sociology classes, including Sociology 101. This was August of 2001. Two weeks later, the Twin Towers in New York were struck down by terrorists. I remember waking up to several calls on my cell phone and pager. When I turned on the news it was surreal. I had never seen or imagined anything that heinous ever happening in the United States let alone New York. I got dressed and went to school that morning, only to be sent home. The whole country was in shock. I thought about my old teammates from West Point that graduated and would be heading to war as commissioned officers. I too wanted to be an honorable person in the community, so this made me determined to succeed.

Living for three years without a plan or a goal produced nothing worthwhile in my life, and had to change. I now had a goal, and that was to get back into San Jose State. There was no way I was going to leave the Bay Area without my bachelor's degree. So the following semester, I buckled down and kept my goal in sight. I went to class every day, and completed every assignment with due diligence and precision.

When the end of the Fall 2001 semester came, I had completed the semester with a 3.8 GPA. All was well until I found out I was going to the wrong class.

Excited to get my report card and then get back into San Jose State I was hit with yet another obstacle. This time it wasn't an eviction, it was the fact that I had been going to the wrong Sociology class the entire semester. I did all the work and even received an 'A' in the class. On my report card though, it showed that I dropped the class. Worried and a little distressed, I went up to Laney College to report the mishap and find out what possibly could have went wrong. The counselor said that I had been dropped from my Sociology class for never showing up. I told her I never missed a day. That's when we found out I was going to the wrong class. Are you kidding me, how could I go to the wrong class for a whole semester and no one know? They informed the professor of the class that I did go to and he advised them that he had all my work and confirmed that my attendance was perfect. I had to petition the Alameda Community College District to get the grade. This process took an entire semester to resolve.

Anxiety

I'd like to rewind a little bit back to November of 2001. Living in Oakland and working in San Jose turned out to be my breaking point. One of the most consistent parts of my life in 2001 was my job renting cars at the airport. I was working 3:30 pm to Midnight. I would take classes in the morning then hit Interstate 880 south to San Jose to go to work. I had been doing this all semester when something strange occurred.

It was common practice for me, on a Wednesday, to meet up with my frat brother who also got off at midnight, hit the Brass Rail strip club for about an hour to have a drink, and then head back to Oakland. This particular night, I had a couple of espressos while waiting for him to get off work. Once he was off, we hit the 101 North to Sunnyvale to make our appearance at amateur night at the Brass Rail. I was there for about an hour and had one drink when I decided I was going to go ahead and leave to get back to Oakland. I said my goodbyes and hit the highway.

I hit the 237 East to the 880 North as I normally did. As soon as I hit the 880 my body started feeling strange and nervous. I was beginning to get dizzy and nervous. I couldn't explain this occurrence and was scared. I was in the fast lane and I immediately started to move over into the slower lanes because my mind and body were feeling so weird. I pulled over to drink some water. Perhaps I was dehydrated and I was just tripping, like people did from lack of water. During the way home, I stopped several times to drink water and get fresh air in the late November night. I would think I was okay when it all started over again as I entered back onto the freeway and hit the fast lane. It was a feeling of helplessness, dizziness, and delusion. I was terrified. It had taken me well over an hour to get home when it normally only took 30-40 minutes. I told myself I would be better in the morning as I pulled up to the house in Oakland.

The next morning I woke up, getting ready to head to Richmond, California near Berkeley. I was going there to get my hair braided by my home girl. I woke up hoping that this mind trip that I had the night before was over and wouldn't continue. As I hit the 580 West towards the 80 East to Richmond, I was nervous and a little faint, but managed to make it to her house. I didn't know what was going on and it wasn't making any sense. Was I going crazy? Had I finally reached the point in my life when I mentally tapped out? I kept asking myself these questions as she was braiding my hair. I kept asking her for water, just in case I was dehydrated and needed to nurse myself back to a clear head. I drank several cups of water before leaving to head back to Oakland.

As I hit the 80 East back to the 580 traffic flowed and I stayed to myself in the right lane. When it was time to merge back onto the 580 going east to Oakland, traffic slowed down and I had to get all the way over into the fourth or fifth lane. Everything moved slowly. My mind was cloudy and my heart was starting to beat at an abnormal pace. It was overcast outside, which is normal for Berkeley in November. The feeling was surreal and different. As I approached the onramp for the 580 an ever-increasing panic came upon me. As the freeway led me onto the 580 in the fast lane, my body went numb. My mind then followed my body. I had a feeling of someone with their hands tied; who had no control. I started to see blue and yellow dots in my eyes. This blurry, dotted vision reminded me of when I passed out at football practice my junior year. I felt as if I was slowly slipping away.

As the sound from outside and inside the truck began to muffle, I began to panic even more. It was like being thrown off a bridge, suspended in air. Not knowing what was going to happen, I only knew that I didn't want to die. I knew that I had more to live for. I thought about my mom and dad, sister and brothers in those split seconds. Traffic was heavy and moving fast coming from the Bay Bridge. My panic was causing me to feel myself passing out. I had to do something fast. I wasn't going to give up. To my left was a black SUV going pretty fast, I slowed down and got behind it. With nothing left to do, I slowed down to a complete stop in the fast lane of the 580 Freeway. Sweating about the palms and face, heart racing, body shaking, and mind blown, I was alive, but changed forever. I had experienced a major panic attack, a form of anxiety, which would haunt me the rest of my days.

The next day I went to the hospital and tried to describe to the doctor what was going on. He asked me if I was on any type of drugs. I told him no. They ran EKG's, did blood tests, a urine test, everything. He basically told me that nothing was wrong with me and it was all in my mind. It's not the best feeling in the world when no one understands what you're going through, and you think you're possibly going crazy. It was another blow to my morale. Kicked out of school watching others graduate, evicted and having to relocate, and now this craziness. All of it caused me to go back into a depression.

From that point on, driving was no longer second nature. It always came with anxiety and stress attached. Whether I was driving on surface streets or the freeway, it was a task. It was scary and horrible to have to drive and experience these crazy feelings. I often felt like my truck was flipping upside down, which caused me to hold on to the steering wheel super tight and lean the other way. I was frantic when I had to go through stoplights or turn left. Getting on the freeway, the major trigger of anxiety was awful in itself. I was living in Oakland, and working in San Jose where the commute was long. For several weeks I had to endure this drive of torture, often exiting the freeway to get a breath of fresh air. I felt as if my world was crumbling.

Being tortured every day by the commute to San Jose, I had no choice but to move back to San Jose. While I waited for the paperwork form Laney to come stating that I did in fact have an "A" in the Sociology class, I enrolled into San Jose City College to stay focused on school and not fall into another rut of inactivity. Spring 2002 I attended San Jose City College and rented a room off of the Interstate 280 Bird Street exit near downtown San Jose. This would be a shorter drive to work and close to campus. Even though I was closer to everything, just driving through the city streets proved to be a challenge on most days. I began to drink heavily to numb my brain from the anxiety and frustrations that came with my panic attacks. Drinking heavily seemed to help relax me in times of stress and anxiety. It was a pseudo way out that was only causing additional problems.

In the fall of 2002, after the paperwork from Laney College came through, I was admitted back into San Jose State University with a second chance. The conditions were that I changed my major. With the encouragement of my mentor, an African American Studies professor at San Jose State, I decided to change my major to African American studies and set a two year goal to graduate. I went to the mental health office at San Jose State and asked to speak with a doctor about my situation. After she offered to put me on drugs, I left and never returned again. Growing up my mother had her share of depression and anxiety and I remembered all the medicine she took over the years. I didn't want that for myself, I wanted to beat it on my own instead of being their test dummy for drugs and side effects. I left the health office and never looked back.

See it Through

In addition to taking my academics more seriously, 2002 is when I started welcoming football back into my life. For years, since the fall of 1997 at West Point, I hadn't watched a game on T.V. or in person outside of visiting Victor Valley to see the "Bell Game." But I started tailgating with my frat brothers at San Jose State games and sometimes Stanford games at this time. I would enjoy the games and seeing these brothers play and then talk to them after the game. It would strike some deep tensions in my heart. It was a joy and a pain all at once.

This is right about the time that I started having very detailed dreams that I was still playing football. I would dream that I was the star player for Army or San Jose State, scoring touchdowns, making tackles, then wake up excited, and enthused that I was playing football again. When I woke up from a football dream it would be like a rebirth. I could feel my blood pumping with passion. It would take me a few seconds to realize that I was in fact tripping. I didn't play football; I gave my dream up years ago and it was over. This was at the same time that I began pondering coaching. I even met with a high school coach in San Jose to talk about helping out with their team. But my plans were derailed when I had a panic attack on the expressway trying to get there. I brushed off the thought of coaching and decided to stay focused on my degree.

I only completed 40 units between entering West Point in 1997 and 2002. I needed 124 units to graduate. My goal was to complete 84 units in two years and be able to walk with the class of 2004. Contrary to the past five years after football, I now had a goal, something to wake up for and strive to achieve. Over the course of those two years I put my nose to the grind and stayed focused. Now that I was back, I vowed to do whatever I had to do to get it done in two years, which included taking 18 or more units per semester. Every semester for two years I loaded up in units. The majority of those classes were my degree and minor classes.

No matter what, I still spent plenty of time with my fraternity brothers. Throughout all the partying and drinking, I still got my class work done. Every Sunday I would wake up early and head to the Martin Luther King Library on campus and just do school work. Sometimes I would go to the African American Studies Department and use the computers there as well. I was proud of myself and my self-esteem was improving despite my anxiety, which at this time continued to play a huge role in my life. At one point I parked my truck and caught the bus to school and walked to work. People wondered why I was walking to work when I had a truck at the house. They couldn't understand that yes I had a truck, but the mental stress and strain that it took to drive just across the city was too much for me. I had met my limit. So I got things done the best way possible, utilizing my feet and public transportation.

After working hard for two straight academic years, I was ready to apply for graduation. So excited and proud of myself, I called home and told everyone the good news. My family was so congratulatory and praising. Throughout the hard times and irresponsibility they hadn't lost faith in me. It was now Spring 2004, seven long years after I set out to accomplish my dream of playing college football. I was finally going to graduate and bring home my degree. After giving up on a dream, switching schools, being homeless and damn near losing my mind, everything was coming to fruition. All I had to do was complete my last semester of classes.

Being involved in the hustle and flow, and halfway in the streets all through college, caused me to have a little paranoia. I was always a little worried about getting robbed or going to jail. I would occasionally have these dreams where I was getting raided and hear sirens and police radios. After a while this became routine and I didn't worry about it. If I had a dream about getting raided I would just wake up and shake it off. They had become all too common.

Wednesday morning before graduation, I kept hearing radios and voices, people running through the bushes by my window. I brushed it off being used to the common dream of being raided. When I ran to the window and looked out, to my surprise, I saw Feds and policemen running through my yard. Shortly thereafter, the banging at the door began. My roommate ran out into the hallway. "San Jose PD, open up!" They were yelling as we started to open the door. When the door was opened an inch of the way they barged into the house. Guns pointed at us, they ordered us on our knees. With the quickness we were handcuffed and sat down on the couch. We sat silent as they handed us the search warrant and committed to ram shack the house. As I read the search warrant, there was an ounce of hope because it didn't have my name on it, only our address. I was still scared about what they would find in my room.

They hit our house at about seven in the morning, and my last math final was at 12 noon. I hoped and prayed that I didn't go to jail so I could complete my last final and be on point to graduate. As I sat there thinking about what my mom was going to think, when she found out I was in jail instead of graduating, I cringed with disbelief. Federal agents and San Jose policemen were going through everything in our house. They kept finding things of interest in my room and walking it out in plastic bags. This was making me nervous. They found my gun that I had since the summer of 1998 and questioned me about it. I said I bought it off the streets years ago. They sat me back down on the couch. In the end, they confiscated trees, scales, and my computer. Fortunately, they didn't find my stash that I had strategically hidden.

When it was all over they didn't find anything they were looking for in relation to their fraud case, and I still had time to get to my final. Luckily I passed.

My mother got to town on Friday. I took her to dinner and then put her up in a hotel while myself and my 2001 neo went to throw the Black Graduation party for San Jose State. I had put up about $4000 for that party. I ended up losing money. The next day, hung over but happy to be free, I threw on my cap and gown and headed to San Jose State for the African American Studies department commencement. Eyes red, still drunk from the night before, I drove the car with my proud mom and my frat brother with me. With pride, I lined up to enter Washington Square Hall with the other graduates.

It had been seven long years. My class of 2001 had graduated three years ago. My road had been long and treacherous, full of ins and outs, ups and downs. It started with a dream of playing football, took an unbelievable turn for the worse, through the hills and valleys and now here I was. When the lady giving the commencement speech started talking passionately about the road to success, and how we've all individually endured to get here, I had no choice but to shed some tears. Her speech hit me so hard in my heart I almost choked. Lucky to be a graduate, even luckier to be sitting in the graduation instead of a jail cell. I was dearly touched. As the tears ran from my eyes, I tried to smile with joy in appreciation of my accomplishment. When I walked the stage setting it out with some traditional hops, and listening to my neo bark and my mother shout with joy, one of the best feelings of my life went through my veins. On May 29th, 2004 I was awarded my Bachelor of Arts in Afro-American Studies with a minor in Sociology.

I realized this was the result of focus and perseverance. I could have backed down and given up at any point during any one of my hardships, but I kept going. **Focus and perseverance is what my bachelor's degree means to me –the ability to set your sights on something and have courage through adversity until you obtain it.** My bachelor's degree was a perfect example of "Seeing it through."

Chapter 9

From Whence I Came

Grateful for my degree, but scared straight from the raid by the police, I moved back home at the beginning of August in 2004. I had just attended our Grand Conclave in St. Louis, Missouri. Anxiety was still an issue for me at this time so I bought my brother a ticket so that he may help me drive back to San Bernardino. He flew up on a Saturday afternoon, and we drove back that Sunday. He dared me to drive half the way, nervous and still suffering from anxiety, I accepted his challenge and we were off. I drove down the 101, to the 152, to the 99 freeway. When we passed Fresno, I was done.

He took over the rest of the way. It was so damn hot coming through Bakersfield and Tehachapi. All of our bottles of water had turned steaming hot from the hot air blowing into the truck. The truck had no air conditioning. I never thought about having AC until it was summertime. Mid-August, going through the Mojave Desert is a haze in itself, let alone without air conditioning. It took us all day to get to Victorville. We stopped by my dad's house to say hello and visit for a while. My final stop would be San Bernardino, at my mother's house. As we crept around the Cajon Pass coming down the 15 Freeway you could see the smoggy Inland Empire. It was the same scene that I often was excited to see as a kid when I was on my way down the hill to visit my mother. This time, coming around that bend meant something different. It represented **a new life and a new journey**. I got goose bumps thinking about the future.

I didn't have a plan, which is never good, but I did know that I wanted to coach football. It had been seven years and my passion was starting to take over my body and soul again. The dreams, the fantasies of still playing were taking their toll and I knew that I had to go with my passion. The best way to feed this void would be by giving back to young boys in the same area that I grew up in. I decided that as soon as I touched down, I would go to the same high school that I played freshmen football at, Rialto High School, and try and get a coaching job. **Coaching would serve as therapy for my past and help me guide other young men in the right direction.**

The next day, a Monday, I went to the high school and asked to speak with the head football coach. Dressed in a frat shirt and some jeans, excited as all get out, I followed the directions they gave me to the classroom he was in. The head coach was a young Latino guy, excited and enthusiastic. I asked him about coaching positions and he did what every coach does and proceeded to ask about my football resume. Every coach has a football resume. Your football resume starts with where you played high school football and who you played under. From there it goes to college. A few lucky people can add the NFL team they played for and then whatever teams you have coached for. At this point in my life, all I had on my resume was freshmen football at Rialto High School, where we were standing, started varsity football three years at Victor Valley High School, and from there I played one season at Army. I ran it off to him with confidence.

He looked at me and said, "You played at Army?" My ambition was to coach varsity defensive backs and running backs. I had been out of the football loop for seven years though and he realized this. He said he could use me on the JV level. I would be matched up with an older gentlemen, well known in Rialto and a world history teacher, who was actually the head coach of the varsity football team when I was a freshmen in 1993. It was an honor to be able to coach with this man. I took the job on that very same day.

I still worked hard at trying to attack my anxiety with full force and determination. It had been so bad while in San Jose that I completely stopped driving for a while. I knew that this was not possible in the Inland Empire because the transportation system wasn't nearly as thorough as it was in the Bay Area. I would be putting myself to a great disadvantage if I wasn't driving. During this time, I worked on overcoming my fear of driving through traffic lights, making left hand turns, and driving on the freeway. Feeling like my life could end at any moment, I persisted. I even bought a self-help program for anxiety to help me beat it. I was able to get better on the city streets, but my fear of the freeway was overwhelming. After forcing myself to drive the freeway to Los Angeles a few times, I relented, and stuck to the streets.

During that football season my mother encouraged me to take the CBEST, a test for educators, so that I may be able to qualify for substitute teaching. So, I signed up for the test and started preparing. I took the test at Cal State San Bernardino, and passed. It was nearing the end of the semester and the school districts said they wouldn't be hiring any more subs until Christmas break, so I waited patiently. Meanwhile, I was still coaching the JV team. The football season started off rocky for our JV team but we ended up winning four games and losing six. The highlight of the season was the last game of the season when we played Eisenhower High School, our cross-town rival. With seconds left in the game, up by a couple points, Ike was driving in towards our goal line. We couldn't seem to stop them. In the final seconds, their coach decides to throw the ball instead of keep running, my strong safety picks the ball off in the end zone to end the game. The kids were going bananas. It reminded me of our win over Apple Valley in the 1994 Bell Game. The memories and the stories, the leadership and the motivation that came from coaching were like soup for my soul.

It really had a positive affect on my life.

In the year 2005 I decided that I wanted to be a teacher. Most of the coaches were teachers. I specifically wanted to be a teacher because I had aspirations of becoming a head football coach. All through high school and college, I often admired how my high school coaches had positive impacts on so many young men. My high school head coach always preached mental toughness and a hard work ethic. Even through my troubled years, I still remembered these lessons that he made us internalize through hard practices and a commitment in the classroom and weight room. These same lessons helped me finally receive my degree and put myself in the position to share my story with young men who were in similar situations like myself.

The next year I started a credential program that included a Master of Education, offered at National University's San Bernardino campus. It would be a 15 month program at the end of which I would be awarded a teaching credential and a master's degree, putting me at the top of the chart for incoming teachers as far as pay grade. This would also make me qualified for a head coaching position. So I set out on this journey with fervor and great zeal. I had focus and ambition. I ended up going as far as I could go in the program until I hit a road block.

When I signed up for this program in 2006 I

didn't do my due diligence. I wouldn't be able to proceed without passing the CSET examination. All of my regular coursework was complete. I had to complete three more classes and my student teaching, but was not qualified to take these classes without first passing this test. Science teachers, in urban schools, are at a high demand so I decided to take the test in Earth Science. I downloaded several study guides and borrowed textbooks to try and conquer this test. I studied hard, I felt very confident about it and went in to take the test. When I opened the test up, it seemed like a foreign language. It was as if I studied the wrong content. I dug my way through the three tests, only to find out a month later that I had only passed one of them. So, I started studying again.

I took these test two years straight without passing. It continued to look as if I would never get a teaching position. But at least I still had my coaching position... or so I thought. I was hit with another bombshell when, due to an altercation over a woman between myself and another guy, this guy wrote a slanderous letter about me to my superiors and the result was my termination. At the time, I had been through so many setbacks in life that I kind of just took it on the chin and accepted it without protest. I would just have to find another job. Feeling wronged and a little devastated, I stopped coaching, applied for unemployment and concentrated on a network marketing business that I was introduced to by my

'97 frat brother, who had risen to the top of the company. I had now shifted my focus to something else.

Network Marketing

Being in network marketing was a daily grind where you had to keep your head right by feeding your brain daily. I started listening to motivational speakers, reading self-help books and everything I could get my hands on about sales and selling. I started to read a whole lot. I probably read more books that year than I did my whole seven years in college. This was all positive literature though and had a huge impact on my energy and ambition. Going to meetings every week, and approaching people I didn't know to take a look at my business was my routine. I had goals and a plan.

Networking events and career expos were common places that I would attend. I met a recruiter for a local after school program at a meet up for Black professionals spearheaded by an ambitious lady from Memphis. This recruiter and I exchanged information, as networkers always do, and I called her to try and recruit her into my business. I didn't know that she was trying to recruit me at the same time for a job at this after school program. When we met at a Starbucks one day I told her what I did, and broke down our compensation plan. She then told me what she did and put it out there that she was looking for people to work with her. I was hired a week later.

During the interviewing process, I noticed a young lady that I had met at Dave and Busters back in 2007 after a football game. In the past, I tried talking to her but she never seemed really interested. I got her attention and spoke to her for a few minutes but respected her time. I told her I was interviewing and would probably end up at Mira Loma Middle School. Turns out the campus she was working at was right around the corner from my campus. She was a happy lady that had just recently graduated the University of California, Riverside and had aspirations to be a lawyer. After I accepted the job and started working, I saw more and more of her. We became real tight and spent a lot of time together. Not long after that we were an item. I loved her ambition and beautiful smile.

The relationship with my future wife was beautiful, but the job itself was horrible. I wasn't successful enough at making sure the average daily attendance at the program was up to par. They pushed me and pushed me about the attendance. I realized that after school programs weren't about helping families and students, it was about money. I tried everything I could to get these students to stay after school, like bribing them with candy and chips, ice cream and fried chicken. Nothing worked and the attendance just went lower and lower. I felt like I was trying my best, but the results weren't sufficient. Finally in May, after just four months of being at that job, I was let go.

In August of 2009, we found out that our first baby was on the way, and would arrive in April of the next year. The thought of marriage seemed great all along, and shortly after the great news, I decided to propose. I drove her up to one of my favorite spots in the mountains that allows you to look over the Inland Empire. All the lights of the Inland Valley in plain sight, I surprisingly handed her a dozen pink roses and watched her gasp for air with surprise in her eyes. As she started to settle down from the shock of the roses, I opened the ring box and showed it to her as I asked her to marry me. She was once again surprised. Crying and fanning herself with excitement, she said yes. We set a date for Valentine's weekend.

When I thought about how I was back on unemployment, had a fiancée and a baby coming, anxiety and pressure started to settle in on my shoulders. My father always preached for us to take care of our responsibilities. I had a plan. Being what I considered well versed in sales due to my job at Alamo, network marketing experience and reading a mountain of books and other literature, I planned on finding a corporate sales job with benefits and a salary. I got word of a career expo at the Green Tree Hotel in Ontario near the airport and planned to attend. I showed up with ambition in my eyes and a smile on my face.

The Rock

Still dealing with anxiety while driving, dating back to the incident on the freeway in 2001, I decided to take the 10 Freeway to Ontario anyway because I tested myself ever so often. Nervous, palms sweaty and a little dizzy, I pulled up to the Green Tree Hotel. I would always sit in the car a few minutes after I arrived somewhere to calm down from the ride there. After I calmed my bad nerves, I jumped out and walked in.

The first booth to my immediate right was a Prudential Insurance booth. As I talked to the recruiter/manager from Prudential, my ambition took over me. I saw unlimited income. I saw Prudential, a well-respected leader in insurance and Fortune 500 company. My ego said it was a good look and match for me. I set up a first interview with the manager and continued browsing. As I browsed I knew I didn't need to look at anymore booths and turned around to go home. All the way home I thought about the income I could make and how my lifestyle would be.

After going through the interview process, composing a list of 200 friends and family members and getting all sorts of background checks completed, I was accepted into the job. It was a one hundred percent commission job, but for the first ten weeks, as I prepared for and took all my licensing, I would be paid a salary. I had to first pass my life and health license, and then I had to pass my Series 6 and Series 63 licenses. By December, I was a fully licensed financial representative and member of FINRA. I was so proud of myself! I wore a suit and tie every day. My family and friends were proud of me outside of the fact that they didn't want me asking them to buy insurance.

The first ten weeks was gravy, but when reality kicked in and the salary stopped, the world changed. The first investment that I wrote was my child's college savings plan. These accounts and other accounts from supportive friends and family would be the easiest money I made. Everything else came hard and with hard work. I would have to pound the phones, which started to get a little repetitive. I went to every business soliciting business owners for group health insurance and life insurance plans. Some days I would walk into 100 stores. It felt like I was walking my life and shoes away. Every now and then, I would hit pay dirt and find someone that was interested and willing to buy.

My first born, my baby girl, came in April of 2010. She was one of the joys that helped counterbalance the everyday stresses I was battling.

The common stresses of being newly married, moving into a new apartment, and hunting for sales was weighing on me. Being a salesman out there in the streets or on the phones, selling things that people don't think they need until they die, is one of the hardest things I've ever done. It made me realize that I wasn't as good in sales as I thought I was, and unfortunately, it made me start drinking a lot more. A couple bottles a day of wine was not unfamiliar during those times I tried to make everything feel better. Though it was only a cover up, and the problems returned as soon as the buzz wore off.

The stress from quotas, and not knowing if you would get a check the next week was taking its toll on me. Sometimes I would get a check for $0.00. At first I thought this was funny, but after a while it was depressing. When I did make a sale, the commission would often go to the negative account that I had from back charges or other deductions that come out of your check. I started to abuse alcohol like I did in college. It never caused me to miss work or do anything irresponsible, but it was still a problem. Sometimes your life is going so fast, but yet so slow that you need a way out. In my situation, alcohol provided a way out. This went on for the extent of my stay at Prudential.

After being at Prudential for two years I was dead broke. I remember walking into Chase Bank to withdraw my last $1000 from my savings account to use for bills that month. When the lady handed me the money, I told her she may as well close that account. By this point, I was also starting to drift into a depressive mood. I was snapping at people at work and really wasn't excited anymore about my job. My hopes and dreams of being a successful insurance and investment professional were slipping away as the days went by. My ego and self-esteem were drifting away as well. My normal 6 feet 185 pound stature had shrunk to a 165 pound frame, and the stress had caused me to have bald spots.

I was at an all-time low, again. It had gotten to a point where while I was watching the movie Rudy with my daughter, I began to cry. I started thinking about my time at West Point and how I had given up on my dreams. If only I could have been more like the character in Rudy with a never say die attitude that my coach had always preached. If only I could have managed to hold myself together and not make an emotional decision to give up my passion and dreams. Where would I be now? It was then that I knew I had to make a change for the better. When you're down, the only thing that's going to get you back up is faith. I had shown a lack of faith at West Point, but I wouldn't show it again. My daughter and family were depending on me.

Pride and not wanting to be called a quitter kept me from quitting Prudential. I didn't know how to let go. My sister told me that sometimes realizing something isn't for you and moving on is not quitting. It took me a long time to accept that message. I could only think about leaving West Point and how the feeling of regret had never left my heart. That in mind, I decided I would find a job to help supplement the lack of income coming from Prudential. After a few weeks of searching the local colleges for advisor jobs, I found myself at the malls applying for sales jobs at jewelry stores. At that point, I was desperate.

Back to Education

After selling jewelry in the Inland Center Mall of San Bernardino for almost a year, things weren't working out. Every month my sales manager would threaten to fire me for not selling enough the month before. My plan was to start coaching and substitute teaching again, then finish my credential/master's program at National University that I started back in 2006. During the last days at Prudential, my sister gave me a great idea. She encouraged me to take the CSET in something easier than earth science so that I may be qualified to proceed with my program. I decided that health science would be one of the easier tests. So, I didn't waste any time to start studying immediately.

In January of 2012, I found out Rialto High School was hiring for a track coach and the season was starting soon. I got together some letters of recommendation from some colleagues and coaches from the past. They were happy to help me out with the letters. I was feeling really good about my recent decision to start back coaching and finish my degree and credential. My life, though still dealing with the jewelry store, was starting to take a turn for the better and I could see some light at the end of the tunnel. Every day before work I would study for my test. I was getting thorough and gaining confidence in taking the health science test.

Then one day, both the head football coach and head track coach from Rialto High School was in the mall and came into my store. He came in to buy something for his wife, and I quickly got his attention and started talking with him. We talked about an hour. I told him how I was trying to get back into coaching football and track, and I would like to coach with him. He said he would like me to join his staff for the spring. He then pointed outside to the head track coach. I went outside the store and talked with the track coach. He also said he could use me as a jump coach. I made two connections that night that proved to me that I was on the right track.

Soon thereafter, I was terminated from the jewelry story, but it was actually a blessing in disguise. This gave me more time to focus on what I really wanted to do. I took the health science test the following week. I took all three tests at once. I felt great about it and knew that I had passed. A month later I received my scores and they were all passing scores. My plan was coming together perfectly. I told my wife, my mom, my brothers and sister, they were all happy to see me making progress and digging myself out of this rut. My dad always used to talk about ruts, how they're easy to get into but hard to get out of. I took my scores down to National University immediately and signed up to finish my program. My mouth was salivating for that credential and master's degree. I was the only one of my siblings left without a graduate degree. My sister was a medical doctor; my oldest brother had a jurist doctorate; and my other brother had a Masters of Business Administration from the famous Drucker School of Claremont Graduate University. I had to make this happen.

The entire fall semester of 2012, while coaching football and substitute teaching, I worked on case studies that had to be completed by October in order to be able to start my student teaching in the spring. I worked endlessly on these case studies. The first one I had to redo because I didn't score high enough. I redid it and over did it at the same time. I finally passed it. The second case study was a cinch using my over do it mentality that I learned from the first. I had them both complete by the deadline and was scheduled to student teach for the spring semester of 2013. My baby boy, my namesake, came a few days later right after we played Pacific High School. He was born on a Saturday afternoon during the Stanford vs. Cal football game, in which Stanford won. I was overjoyed by his arrival, but the fact that he was born during a football rivalry game, made it that much better.

Student teaching would be sixteen weeks of training under a master teacher in which I didn't get paid. Luckily, I saved my whole stipend from football to cover me for the majority of the four months. Student teaching started in January of 2013, and was to be over at the end of the semester in June. During student teaching I had to take a seminar class at the same time. I couldn't miss one day of student teaching and essentially had to take over the class, making lesson plans and grading papers. Every other week I would get evaluated by my National University representative. For sixteen weeks I endured this routine. At the end of the semester I was happy to inform my family that I would be accepting my Master of Education along with my teaching credential at the National University commencement. It brought great joy to my family's hearts and tears of joy to my eyes to be able to announce this honorable event.

It started out as a thought, then as a plan. With some minor setbacks and obstacles, my goal was derailed and put off for years. During those years, I overcame stress and low self-esteem, depression and alcohol abuse, but kept fighting. Often times in life you end up where you don't want to be.

Sometimes you end up where you want to be but don't need to be. It takes a lot to recognize these scenarios. Sometimes you just want to quit, and pity yourself. **A real fighter, a real person of fortitude and perseverance will not give up.** Relentless, they will keep fighting, setting goals and doing all they can to accomplish the little goals that lead to the main goal. Finally arriving at the crux of the whole matter. Life is just a series of projects and obstacles. We must persevere and be steadfast through life while keeping our eyes on the prize.

On May 30, 2013 I walked the stage in San Diego California to receive my Master of Education and teaching credential from National University. Distracted by hard times I lost sight of my new dream, but I never let it die. I let my old dream of playing football in college die. It was reincarnated as a dream to give back to the community as a teacher and a coach. I learned my lesson when it came to giving up on dreams, so even through the different career paths and jobs, I kept my dream alive by making it one of my yearly goals every year. Finally when the time was right, I was able to get back into focus and bring my dream to the forefront. With focus and perseverance, and the support of my wife and family, I proudly accepted my degree.

Best Christmas Gift

Back in 1997 when I left West Point after the football season and semester ended, I never made it back to attend the football banquet held in January of 1998 where they handed out certificates, athletic letters, and other awards. Though I was hurt a majority of the season and wasn't able to suit up for a game and earn a varsity letter, I was entitled to a junior varsity letter for completing the season and being an asset on the scout team after I rehabbed back from my knee injury. I was never able to accept my letter or certificate and the academy never forwarded it to me in California.

Over the years, I started having more pride in my journey to West Point. I wanted my athletic letter to show I was a part of that 1997 Army Football team. After expressing this over the years to my wife, she set out on a covert mission to make this happen. Right before Christmas 2013 a letter showed up to my door from West Point. I opened the letter to see my JV football letter from Army and a copy of a page from the 1997 Army Football Media Guide with my name on it representing Victorville, CA.

After 16 years, I finally was awarded what I knew I deserved back in 1997 –my Army football letter. I was overwhelmed with joy – and some bitterness. The joy of receiving my just due for completing the 1997 season with Army, and the tangible proof that came with it. The bitterness came as a result of the vivid memory of being hurt at West Point and my deflated childhood dream. As I held that JV football letter and Media Guide, I thought about my hard times growing up, my football story and my life in general.

That moment was the moment I decided to share my story with others –to write a book. Learning from my experience should encourage you to **follow your dreams and dare yourself to greatness**. Thank you for allowing me to share my story with you.

Keep Your Eyes on the Prize!

Acknowledgements

A special thanks to...

The Supreme Architect of the Universe!
My editor Georgina Chong-You, for her professionalism and expertise.
My lovely wife and children for supporting my project.
My fearless grandmother "Mommee."
My loving mother.
Dad and Nana.
Jerry Jr., Steven and Stavonnie for setting prime examples.
Jerry III for his major moral support.
Uncle Don for his wisdom.
Uncle Mike for inspiring my football dream.
The 1993 Rialto High School Football Program.
The 1994-1996 Victor Valley High School Football programs.
Coach Art Sanchez
Coach Julian Reddick (deceased)
Mr. Elvin Momon
Mrs. Judy Munoz
Victor Valley High School class of 1997. V-Hi!
97 Hot Boys!
Lamont Smith
Charles, his mother Janet Stinson and Family.
The United States Military Academy at West Point.
The 1997 Army Black Knight Football team.

San Jose State University
Rio Burns
My Dean, Don Aguillard.
The Xi Gamma Chapter of Omega Psi Phi Fraternity, Incorporated.
The Sigma Eta Chapter, "Home of Omega Fest."
Omega Psi Phi Fraternity, Incorporated. F.I.E.T.T.S.
The 99 Family!
Kelvin Smith Sr.
Michael "England" Okoro
My mentor, Brother Dr. Steven Millner.
Laney College of Oakland, CA
San Jose City College
San Jose State University class of 2004.
Orange Valley Lodge #13, MWPHGL F&AM State of California, Incorporated- Travel Light!
National University class of 2013.
Psalms 133
All my friends and family that supported me over the years.

All my friends and family Resting in Peace...
See you when I get there!

In Loving Memory of my Uncle Buck, who passed away in the final stages of this book's completion. May his selfless spirit continue to shine!
1.17.1947 - 2.14.2015